CW01667964

The Ashford Book of

Hand Spinning

The Art of Making Beautiful Yarn

Jo Reeve

Contents

First published in 2009

ISBN: 978-0-9582881-5-6
Printed in China by Everbest Ltd
Published by Ashford Handicrafts Ltd
Ashburton, New Zealand
Email: sales@ashford.co.nz

Welcome to the wonderful world of hand spinning.

Spinning is the delightful art of drawing out fibre by hand to make yarn. Why spin? Perhaps the question should be why not? Hand spinning is more than just making yarn. It is a life-long journey of fun, friendships, creativity and learning. Spinning is wonderfully relaxing and the drafting of fibres onto a spindle or spinning wheel is rhythmic and peaceful.

As the spindle or bobbin fills, there is instant gratification and a sense of excitement and urgency to see the finished yarn.

Spinning yarn for textiles is the perfect way to unleash your creative side. Handspun yarn feels special and has a charm and personality all of its own. Your personality too will be reflected in the yarns you create by the colours and textures you choose to spin.

These days, there is a wonderful range of fibre available for spinning. Most spinners I know have a stash – a big stash of beautiful fibre. Wool, silk, alpaca, mohair, cotton and bamboo to name just a few. Imagine a soft, luxurious yarn of silk, mohair and wool – it would be irresistible to touch. Or perhaps a brightly coloured novelty yarn which twists and turns every which way. The possibilities are endless.

There are many reasons folk like to spin. For some it is about lifestyle and living a dream. They have a great love of the land and put a lot of time into caring for the animals that produce their fibre for spinning – wool from sheep, alpaca fibre and angora from rabbits.

For most of us though, we must purchase our fibre from a shop, or the internet or, if you are lucky, a farmer who lives nearby.

Wherever your fibre comes from, natural fibre for spinning is a renewable resource and a practical way to reduce your carbon footprint.

There is a great sense of achievement to be gained from the "start to finish" aspect of hand spinning. The fibre you spin will be transformed into wonderful yarn and then into a unique product. There will be no other like it.

Or perhaps your dream is to spin a basketful of gorgeous skeins that are simply there to be gazed at or admired every time you pass by.

Spinners are very generous folk and like nothing more than to share their knowledge with new spinners. On your journey through the spinning world, you will form many wonderful friendships that will last a lifetime.

For me, spinning has become a life-long passion. The anticipation of starting a new project, spinning a different fibre, or blending an unusual colour combination, keeps that passion strong. It will never fade.

I feel privileged to have been given the opportunity to share with you the knowledge I have accumulated over the past 27 years. I hope you have as much pleasure and fun from spinning as I do and that your life is enhanced by learning this wonderful craft.

Jo Reeve

The process of making yarn by hand spinning is no different than yarn being made in a mill. It is just on a much smaller scale. Spinners usually have lots of questions when they begin. Where did the fibre come from? How was it processed for spinning? What happens after I have spun the fibre? Here is a description of each step you will learn in this book to make beautiful yarn.

Fibre for spinning

Almost any fibre can be spun into yarn. Fibre falls into two main categories for spinning – animal and vegetable. Animal fibres generally comprise proteins and include fibre such as wool, silk, alpaca, mohair, angora and camel. Vegetable fibres are made up of cellulose and some examples are cotton, bamboo, flax, hemp and Tencel.

Wool is the most common fibre used by hand spinners and is perfect for learning to spin. It is the natural winter coat, or fleece, of a sheep. A sheep does not need its heavy, woolly warmth during the hot summer months so it is harvested by shearing, usually in spring when the coldest of winter days have passed.

Wool comes in two forms for hand spinning. Raw fleece, which can be spun washed or unwashed, and sliver (also called roving), which is commercially prepared wool ready for spinning. Either form is fine for a new spinner. Some spinners like to work with fibre in its natural state whereas others prefer it washed. It is simply a matter of personal preference.

If you have decided to start with fleece, read the information about wool on page 49 to help you make a choice.

Fibre preparation

Fibre that has been untangled and opened up is easier to spin. This is called carding and can be done using a variety of tools. For a beginner using fleece, a flick carder is the ideal tool with which to start.

Once the basic spinning and carding skills have been established, more advanced tools such as hand carders and a drum carder can be used to process the fibre in many different ways.

Spinning

The carded fibre is drawn out (drafted) and spun into a continuous thread onto either a spindle or spinning wheel. Different types of yarns can be spun using different drafting methods.

Plying

To give yarn strength, most handspun threads are plied by twisting two or more threads together in the opposite direction to that of the spinning. Plying also removes some of the twist from each thread which creates a more balanced yarn.

Finishing

The plied yarn is wound into a skein and then washed to set the twist. Now the yarn is ready to be made into a beautiful textile.

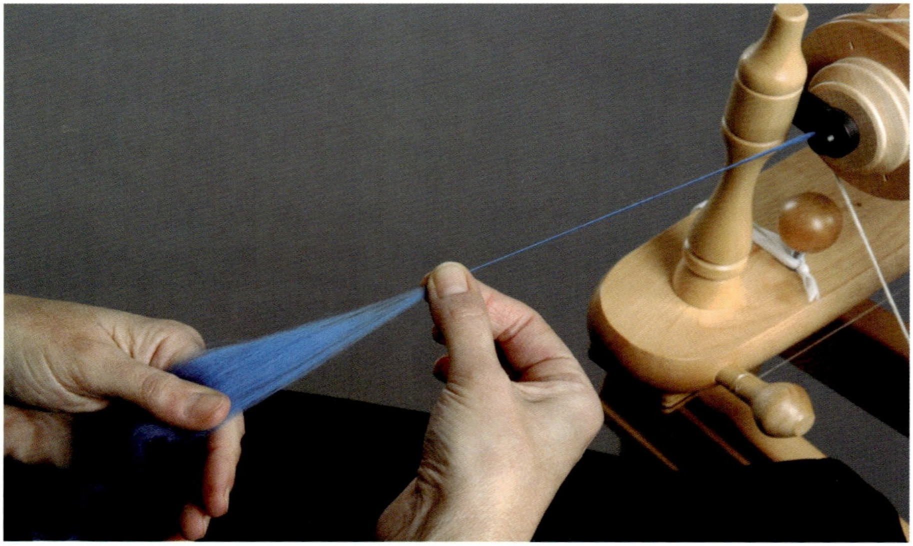

Pinching to control the twist entering the unspun fibre

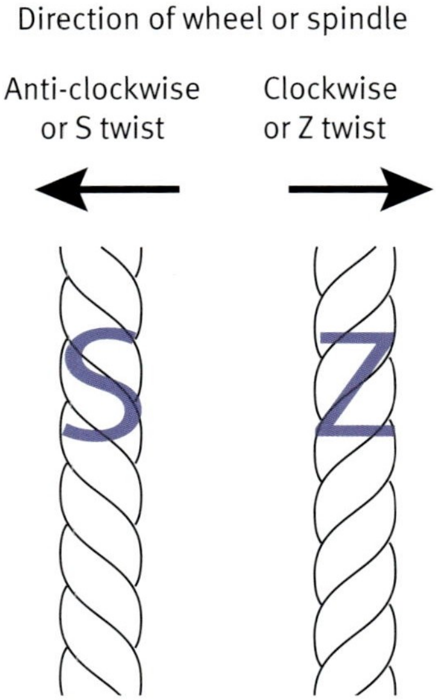

A new spinner has a lot to think about as he or she sets out on this new journey. There are many skills and spinning terms to learn so it's a good idea to familiarise yourself with some 'spinning talk' before you begin. Here are some terms that will help you in the early stages.

Drafting

Drafting is the process of drawing out a measured amount of unspun fibre in order to produce an even, consistent yarn when spun. If undrafted fibre is spun the yarn will quickly become too bulky and unmanageable. To avoid this problem, the thumb and finger of one hand will pinch and relax to control the amount of twist entering the unspun fibre. The other hand will hold and draft the fibre.

Drafting zone

The is the area between the two hands. The amount of fibre in this area determines the thickness of your yarn. To spin a consistent diameter yarn, you will need to concentrate on the drafting zone, not the spun yarn.

Staple

A staple is an individual lock. Fibres with a long staple can be drafted out further than fibres with a short staple. To get a feel for how far the fibres can be drawn out before they separate, practise drafting as described on the next page.

Twist direction

Your spun yarn will have a twist direction. When the spindle or wheel turns clockwise, the yarn has a Z twist and when it turns anti-clockwise, it has an S twist. The first stroke of each letter as you would write it, is the direction the wheel or spindle is turning and the angle in the centre of each letter is similar to the angle in the spun fibre. It's a good idea to know your twist directions. They will come in very handy when you are ready to make plied yarns.

Single

Each spun yarn is called a single. It can be used on its own or plied.

Drafting

Some spinners find it useful to practise drafting before they begin spinning. In the photographs I will refer to the hand controlling the twist as the 'front' hand, and the drafting hand as the 'back' hand. Experiment using either your left or right hand as the front hand and use whichever feels the more comfortable and natural for you.

The hand holding the fibre needs to be very relaxed to allow the fibre to flow easily into the drafting zone.

Using a staple of fleece or a small piece of sliver, hold the fibre very loosely in your back hand with your thumb on top. Draw out a few fibres from the end with your front hand and, keeping hold of them fairly firmly, rest this hand on your lap. Your hands should be about 5cm (2ins) apart.

Keeping your front hand stationary, put a little pressure on the fibre with the thumb of your back hand and gently draw the fibre back, about 5cm (2ins). Move your front hand closer to your back hand so your hands are once again about 5cm (2ins) apart and craft again. Keep on doing this until you reach the end of the fibre. You should have a long, airy strip of wool.

Hold the fibre with your hands 25-30cm (10-12ins) apart and use the thumb and index finger of your front hand to twist the wool in a clockwise direction. This is the work the spindle or spinning wheel will do for you. Now try pulling it apart. You will feel the strength that has been introduced by the twist.

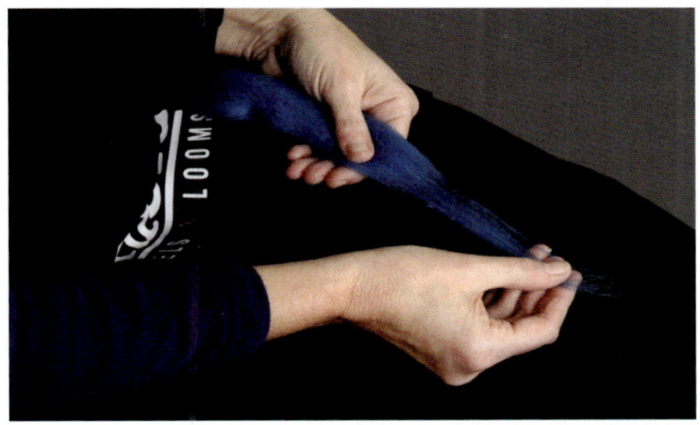

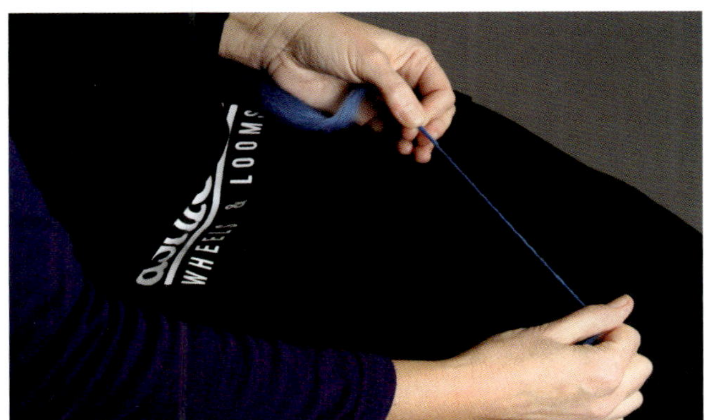

Top Whorl Drop Spindle

Hand spinners can use either a drop spindle or a spinning wheel to spin. Both tools are very productive means of making yarn and the principle of spinning is the same. There are many types of spindles and wheels available, providing spinners with a wonderful range of tools able to produce a variety of handspun yarns.

Drop spindle

A drop spindle is a delightful, small hand tool which predates the spinning wheel. It comprises a shaft, usually made from wood, weighted at one end with a circular whorl which keeps the spindle turning.

A drop spindle is suspended by the yarn. It usually has a small hook or notch, either in the whorl or the shaft, to secure the yarn. A spindle with the hook at the top of the shaft and the whorl at the bottom is known as a bottom whorl spindle and when the hook and whorl are at the top, it is a top whorl spindle.

The Ashford Traditional Spinning Wheel

Spinning wheel

The spinning wheel still uses a spindle but it is foot-driven. The hands are free to spin continuously. The fibre is twisted and wound onto a bobbin in one action.

The flyer and bobbin are supported by two posts called maiden uprights. For a complete description of all the spinning wheel parts, refer to page 100.

The bobbin slides onto the flyer

The advantages of using a spindle cannot be ignored. As well as being affordable, efficient and cute, it is incredibly portable – a tool that allows you to spin any place, any time.

Rotating the spindle

A length of yarn called the leader is needed to anchor the unspun fibre when you start spinning. Tie a 45cm(18ins) length of yarn to the spindle shaft, just under the whorl and make a loop at the other end of the yarn using a square knot. Take the yarn up over the whorl and underneath the hook.

Hold the leader with either hand, letting the spindle fall under your hand. Hold the shaft between your thumb and index finger of your other hand and give it a good strong spin in a clockwise direction – Z twist. It should rotate freely and fairly quickly. Practise this several times until you are consistently getting the spindle to start and continue rotating. Now practise rotating it with S twist – anticlockwise.

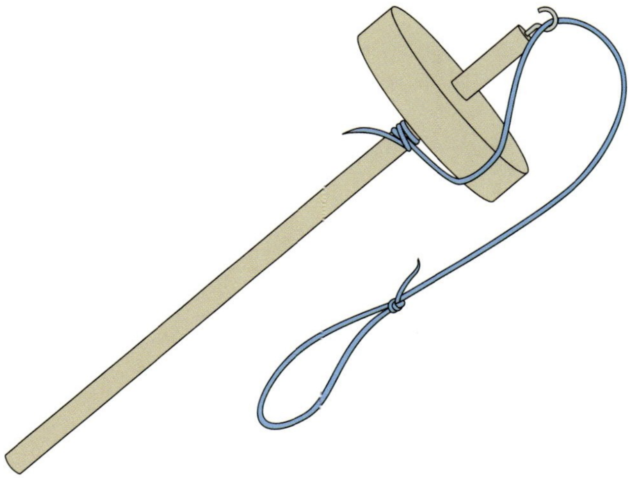

Organise your fibre

If you are using fleece, make sure you have a reasonable quantity prepared so you don't lose your rhythm by having to stop and card fibre. Flick carding is the easiest method with which to start. Read the instructions on page 34 to prepare your staples.

For sliver, you can either pull off staple lengths or divide longer lengths into strips. Wrap a strip around your wrist to prevent it from getting caught in the yarn.

Spinning

Spindle spinning is best done standing up. When you first begin, there will be times when the yarn will break or the drafted fibres will separate and the spindle will fall to the floor. To soften its landing and prevent damage, try spinning over a carpet or rug.

One hand will hold the fibre and control the twist, and the other will do the drafting and spin the spindle. For ease of learning, I will refer to the fibre hand as your top hand, and the drafting hand as your bottom hand.

Hold the fibre very loosely in your top hand. Draw out a few fibres from the end of the staple or sliver and take them through the loop of the leader and back on themselves for 5cm (2ins), pinching the folded ends with your thumb and index finger.

With your other hand start the spindle rotating clockwise (Z twist) and once the folded fibre starts to twist together, move this hand so it is just underneath your top hand ready to start drafting downwards.

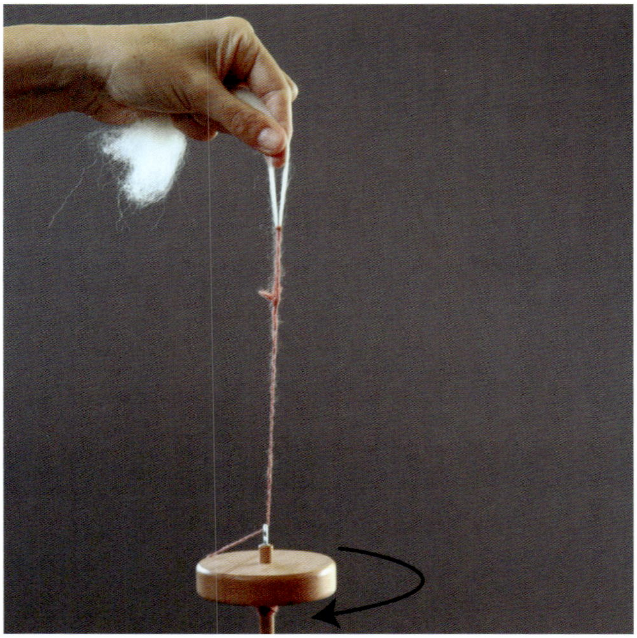

Pinching the folded fibres

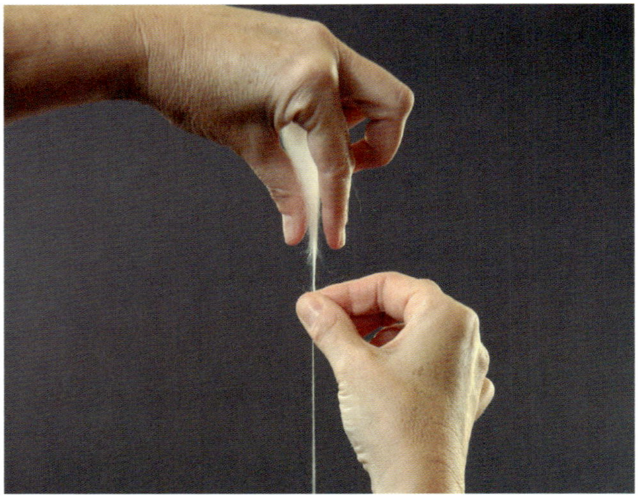

Top hand: Relax, Bottom hand: Draft down

Now release the pinch with your top hand and draft the fibre downwards with your bottom hand. Try and keep an eye on the spindle, watching to see when it slows down. Give it another twirl before it stops completely.

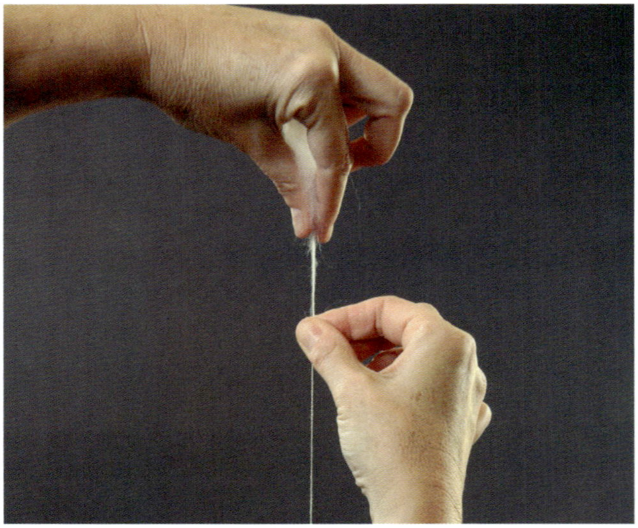

Top hand: Pinch, Bottom hand: Slide up

Pinch the fibre again with your top hand to prevent the twist from entering the fibre supply. Slide your bottom hand thumb and index finger up the twisted fibre and draft again.

Winding on

Winding on

Keep spinning until the length of yarn is about the same as your outstretched drafting arm. Pinch off the twist with your top hand, reach down and catch the spindle with your bottom hand.

Keeping your hands apart to hold the yarn under tension, unhook the yarn and wind on in a clockwise direction, nestling the yarn firmly against the whorl. Rehook, leaving a few centimetres/inches between the whorl and the fibre supply to start spinning again.

Joining in more fibre

Now you're back at the beginning. Your spun yarn is now the 'leader'. Draw out a few fibres from the end of a new staple or piece of sliver, overlap with your spun yarn, pinch it off and start the spindle turning. As the two ends twist together, you can start the rhythm again – relax, draft, pinch, slide up.

Continue spinning until you feel a change in the efficiency of the spindle. As the spindle fills and becomes heavy, it may start to wobble around. This is a good indication that it is full.

How much twist?

There needs to be a good amount of twist in the yarn to make it strong. Just before winding on, check the twist by letting the yarn go slack between the fibre supply and the spindle, allowing it to twist back on itself. The plied yarn should look firm but not hard and there should be no gaps. After some experience your eyes will be the best judge of twist.

Plying

My preferred method is Andean plying. It is fuss free, there is absolutely no waste, there is no tangling and it can be done anywhere, any time. Andean plying is also very useful when making samples from either the spindle or a bobbin.

Andean plying

Andean plying is a very clever method of making a two-ply yarn from a single thread. The way in which the single thread is wrapped around your hand enables the two ends to be unwound without tangling.

If too much yarn is wound at once, it may become too tight and be difficult to remove, not to mention cutting off the blood supply to one or more fingers! To overcome this problem, several 'bracelets' can be stacked on top of each other to keep things manageable.

Secure the end of the yarn by tucking it into your cuff, watch strap or a rubber band. Take the yarn up and behind your middle finger, then down and around the back of your hand (Fig.1). Now bring the yarn up and behind your middle finger, then down and around the back of your hand in the opposite direction (Fig.2).

Repeat until the yarn starts to feel a little tight around your middle finger (Fig.3). The back of your hand should look like Fig.4.

Slip the yarn off your middle finger, sliding it down to your wrist to form a 'bracelet' (Fig.5). Begin winding around your hand again (Fig.6). Slide the second bracelet down to your wrist. Attach the ends to your leader, and you are now ready to ply.

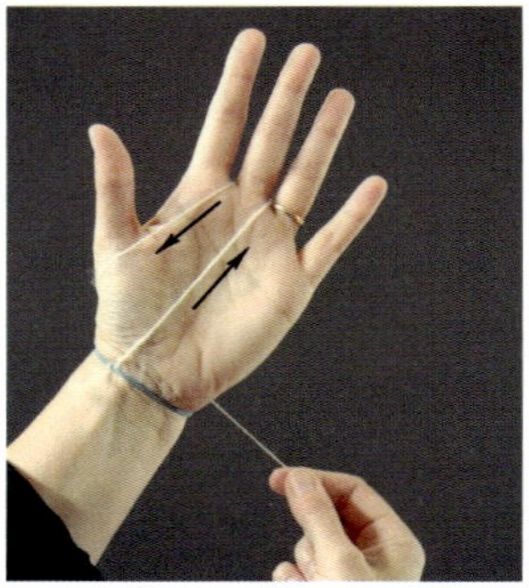

Fig.1

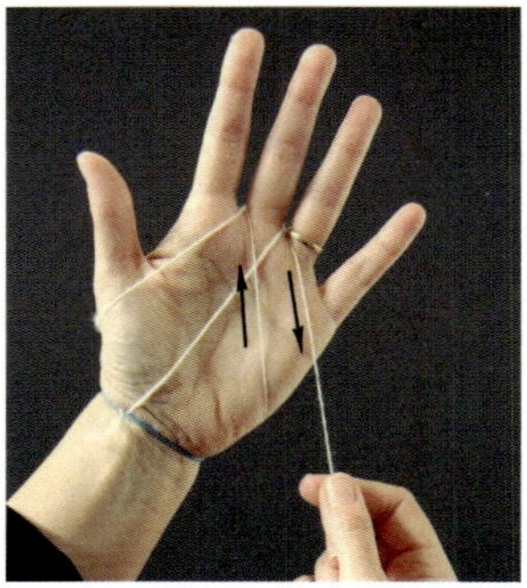

Fig.2

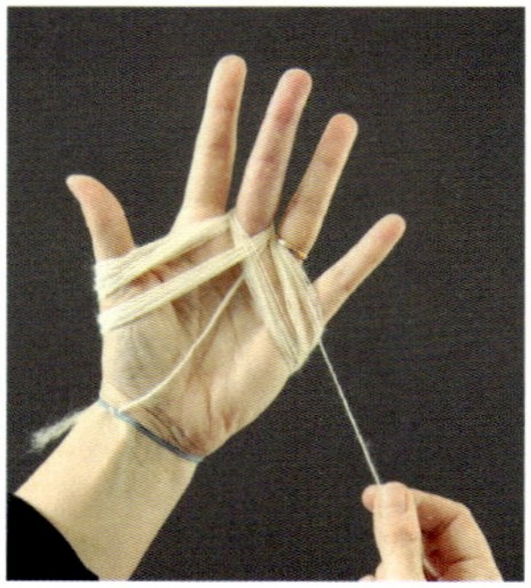

Fig.3

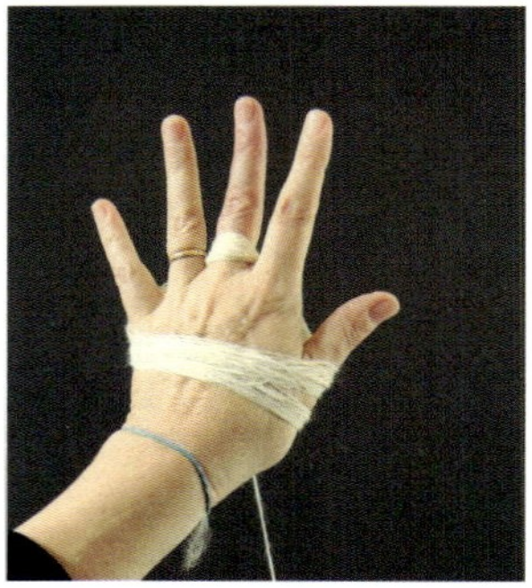

Fig.4

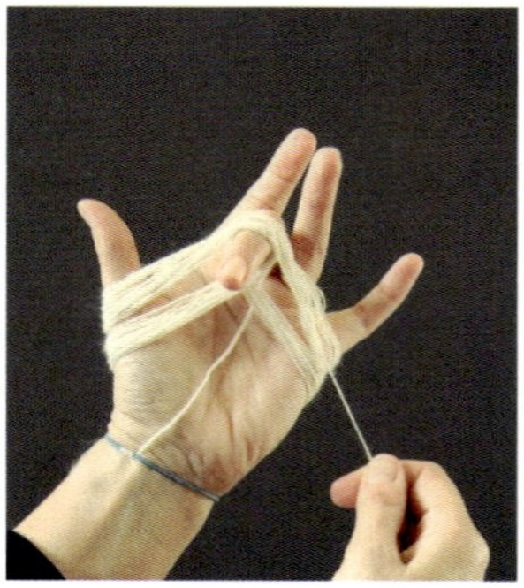

Fig.5

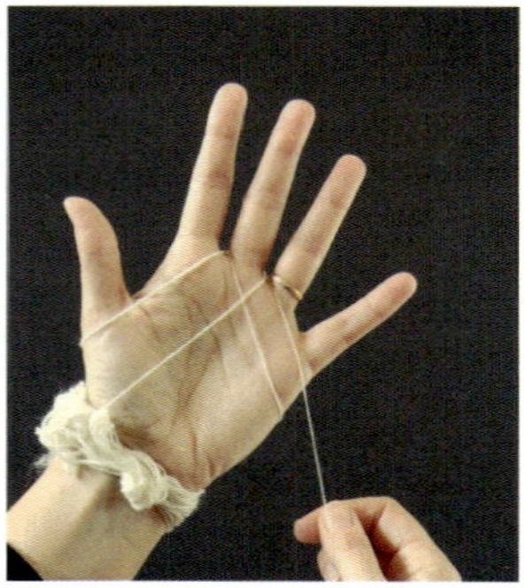

Fig.6

As the yarn was spun Z twist, you will be plying in the opposite direction – anticlockwise or S twist. Take the two ends and thread them through the loop in the leader, folding them back on themselves for about 5cm (2ins) and pinch them together with the thumb and index finger of your top hand.

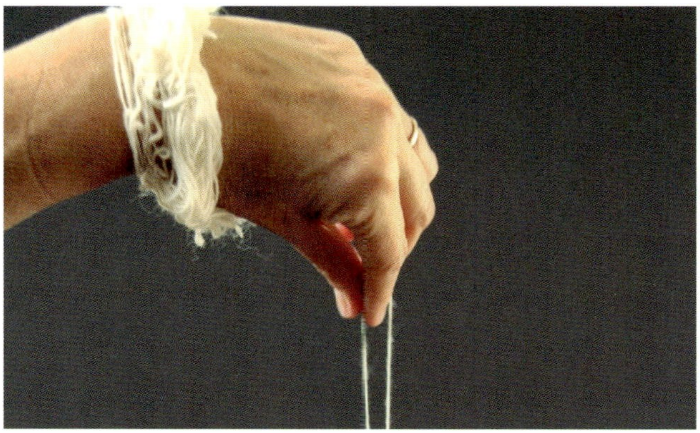

Start the spindle anticlockwise. Let it rotate for several revolutions, watching to see when the folded back ends have twisted around each other. Release the pinch of your top hand and place your index finger between the two singles.

With your bottom hand, draw the two singles down to an arm's length, letting them slide through the fingers of your top hand. Slide your bottom hand thumb and index finger up the plied yarn to within about 5cm (2ins) of your top hand and draw down again.

Plying will be much quicker than spinning so you will need to wind on more regularly.

An alternative to Andean plying is to spin two singles which are wound into balls and then plied as above. The balls can be placed in containers to keep them from tangling or, if you have a ball winder, you can use that to make a centre-pull ball.

Under-plied

Over-plied

Balanced

Making a balanced yarn

When you have plied and wound on 2-3 times, stop the spindle and check for a balanced yarn. Let it relax between your two hands. It should hang straight without any twisting.

If it looks loose and has gaps between the two singles, it is under-plied and needs more twist by either rotating the spindle faster as you ply or giving it another twirl without drawing out any yarn just before you wind on.

If little kinks form along the length of the plied yarn, there is too much twist. Try drawing out more yarn without rotating the spindle. The extra twist will then be distributed along a longer length of yarn.

Finishing

When plying is complete, your yarn needs to be skeined and washed to set the twist. Place the spindle on the floor, wedging it firmly between your feet and wind the plied yarn onto a niddy noddy (see page 24). Tie it off in several places, four should be enough, and remove from the niddy noddy. Set the twist by hand-washing in lukewarm water with a little mild detergent or liquid wool wash.

Getting to know your spinning wheel

There is a lot to think about when learning to spin on a spinning wheel. Coordination of your hands and feet takes a little time to feel natural so take your time and don't worry about trying to make a perfect yarn. To avoid a sore back or shoulders, it is very important to be comfortable and relaxed while you are spinning. Use a chair that supports your back well and try not to crouch over the spinning wheel. Try different chairs until you find the one that most suits your height.

Treadling

It helps a lot if you practise treadling the wheel before you actually start spinning with fibre. With large diameter wheels like the Traditional or Elizabeth, a single treadle is relaxing and easy to use with one or two feet on the treadle. On smaller diameter wheels, like the Kiwi or Traveller, two treadles ensure a constant speed is maintained.

You will need to work slowly while you are learning. Use the largest whorl on your flyer as this gives you the slowest speed.

Place your foot, or feet on the treadle(s) and start treadling. If the crank is at its lowest or highest position, you may need to start the wheel by hand. With your fingers resting on one of the drive wheel spokes, give the wheel a push in a clockwise direction. Keep the wheel going by treadling slowly and steadily with a heel to toe action – about one treadle for each second. To prevent the wheel slipping, push down with your foot rather than away.

Once you get a feel for using the treadle, slow down your treadling and stop when the crank is at 1 o'clock. Now try starting the wheel just with your foot. Once you feel comfortable treadling clockwise, try starting the wheel going in an anti-clockwise direction. This time, slow down your treadling and stop the wheel at 11 o'clock. Start the wheel again using just your foot, treadling slowly and steadily.

Practise treadling in both directions until you can start and stop the wheel at will.

Relaxed and comfortable at the wheel

Setting up your wheel

There are two main systems of spinning – the single drive (Scotch tension) or double drive system. There is a third, less common, system called bobbin lead (Irish tension).

These systems introduce a difference in speed between the flyer and bobbin. This difference allows the yarn to wind onto the bobbin.

Single drive

Double drive

Bobbin lead

Single drive (Scotch tension)

The flyer is driven by the drive band and the yarn pulls the bobbin around. The brake band is used to slow the bobbin slightly.

The drive band: Runs around the groove in the drive wheel and over the largest groove in the flyer whorl.

The brake band: Check that it is wrapped around the tension knob two or three times. Place the band over the large bobbin whorl and connect the spring to the hook on the other side of the maiden. Turn the tension knob until the brake band is tight and the two springs are just about to stretch.

Double drive

The drive band drives both the flyer and bobbin. As the flyer and the bobbin have different size whorls they are driven at different speeds.

Wrap the drive band around the groove in the drive wheel, around the large flyer whorl, back around the wheel and around the bobbin whorl.

To convert to single drive, place both drive bands (or one new drive band) over one groove in the flyer whorl. Install and place the brake band over the bobbin whorl.

Bobbin lead (Irish tension)

The drive band drives the bobbin instead of the flyer. The drive band goes around the drive wheel and bobbin whorl. The brake band runs over the flyer whorl.

The Ashford Country Spinner uses the bobbin lead system and all Ashford double drive wheels can be converted to this system.

Drive band tension – All systems

There need only be enough tension to drive the flyer and/or bobbin without slippage. Too much tension makes treadling harder. Test the tension by pressing your finger on the drive band. You should be able to easily depress it about 25mm (1in).

Setting up the leader

Bobbin tension

A length of yarn called the leader is needed to anchor the unspun fibre when you start spinning. Tie a 1m (3ft) length of knitting yarn firmly onto the empty bobbin. Place the bobbin on the spindle and click the spindle back into the bearing. Thread it around the hook near the orifice and then through the orifice using the threading hook. Make a loop at the end of the leader.

Perfect tension is the key to relaxed and easy spinning. Only use enough tension to just draw in the yarn. On a single drive wheel the tension knob is very sensitive and will require only the smallest movement to make a difference. Hold the leader about 15-20cm (6-8ins) away from the orifice and start treadling.

Perfect: If the leader slides gracefully through your fingers, through the orifice and winds onto the bobbin your tension is perfect.

Too tight: If it is pulled out of your hands and disappears out of sight, the tension is too tight. Loosen it a little, re-thread your leader to test the tension again.

Too loose: If the leader did not pull in at all and twisted back on itself in front of the orifice, the tension is too loose. Tighten it a little and test the tension again.

It is worth spending some time getting a feel for the tension adjustments. Try starting with it very loose and gradually tighten the tension until the leader just pulls in.

Spinning

Organise your prepared fibre beside you on a small table or in a basket. A continuous supply will help you establish a good rhythm. While you are learning, it is best not to stop often to prepare more fibre.

A good, easy to spin fibre to start with is the Ashford Corriedale sliver. Divide it into lengths of approximately 30cm (12ins) to keep the amount of fibre manageable. If you have decided to start with fleece, flick card the staples following the instructions on page 34.

Protect your clothing with an apron or cloth. It's good to be able to see the fibre clearly against a contrasting colour as you draft. I use a medium weight cotton cloth which is black on one side and white on the other. It's ideal for any fibre colour.

At this stage it does not matter from which end of the fibre you spin. If your yarn breaks or becomes too thick to pass through the orifice, break it off and start again.

The technique described on the following pages is called the 'short backward draft'. There are certainly other spinning techniques which you will want to explore as you become more confident and these are described on pages 28-33. This drafting method is your starting point and soon you will develop your own style.

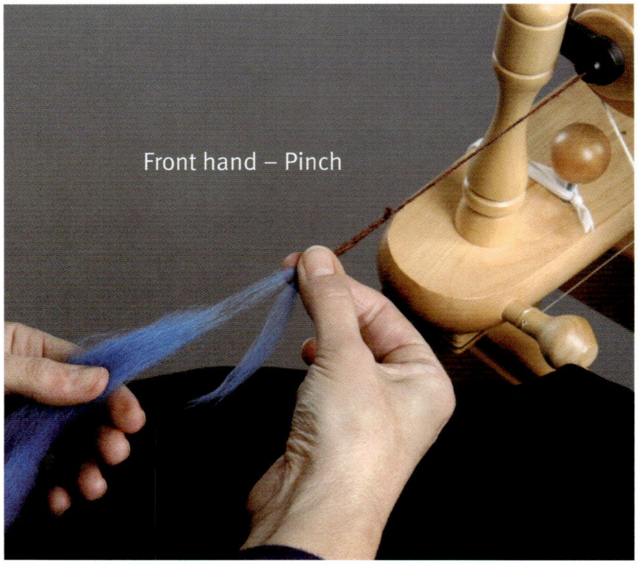

A pinch of fibre

Treadle the spinning wheel slowly in a Z twist direction (clockwise) until about 20-25cm (8-10ins) of the leader is left hanging out of the orifice.

Take your first staple or portion of sliver and draw out a few fibres from the end. Thread them through the loop of the leader, fold back and pinch with your front hand.

Hold the fibre loosely in your back hand. Keep this hand *very* relaxed and try not to clutch the fibre.

In the zone

Start treadling slowly, still in a Z twist direction. As soon as you see the fibre start to twist, draft the fibre back towards your body with your back hand. Do not worry about lumps and bumps at this stage.

Watch the drafting zone between your hands as you are spinning.

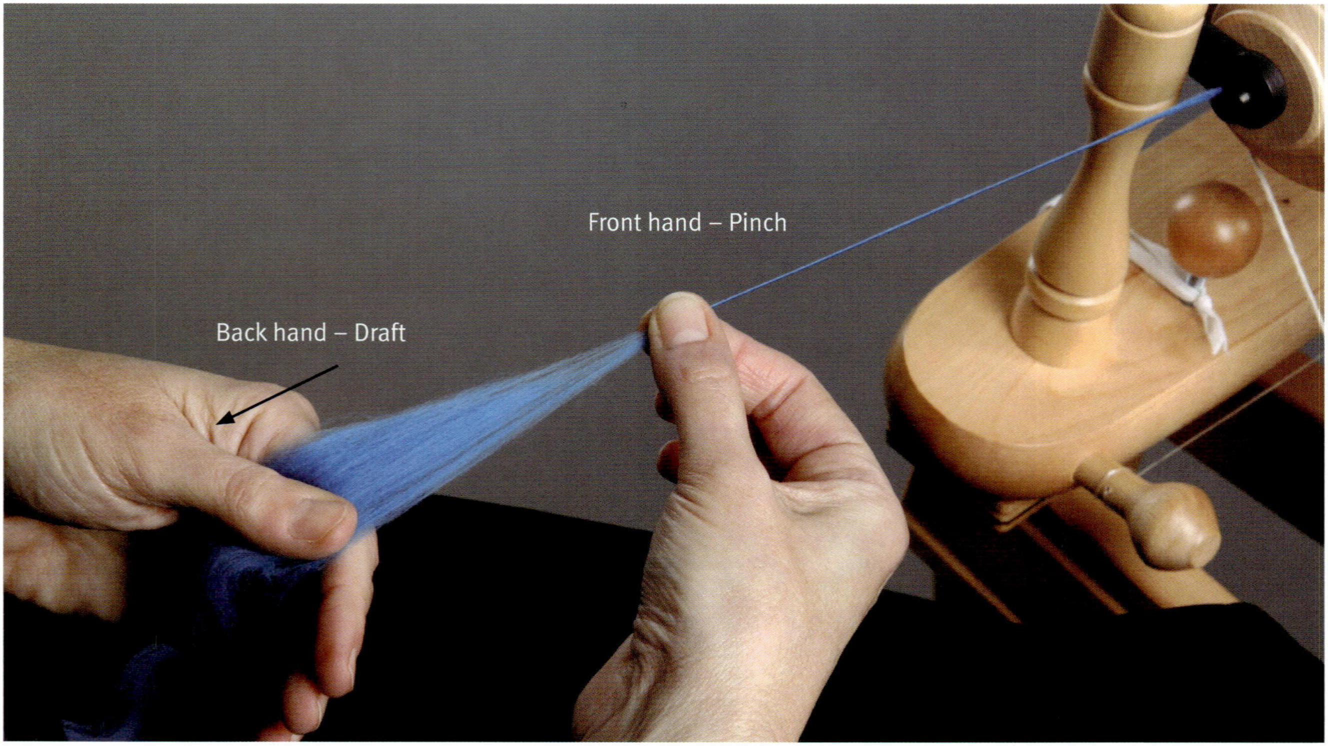

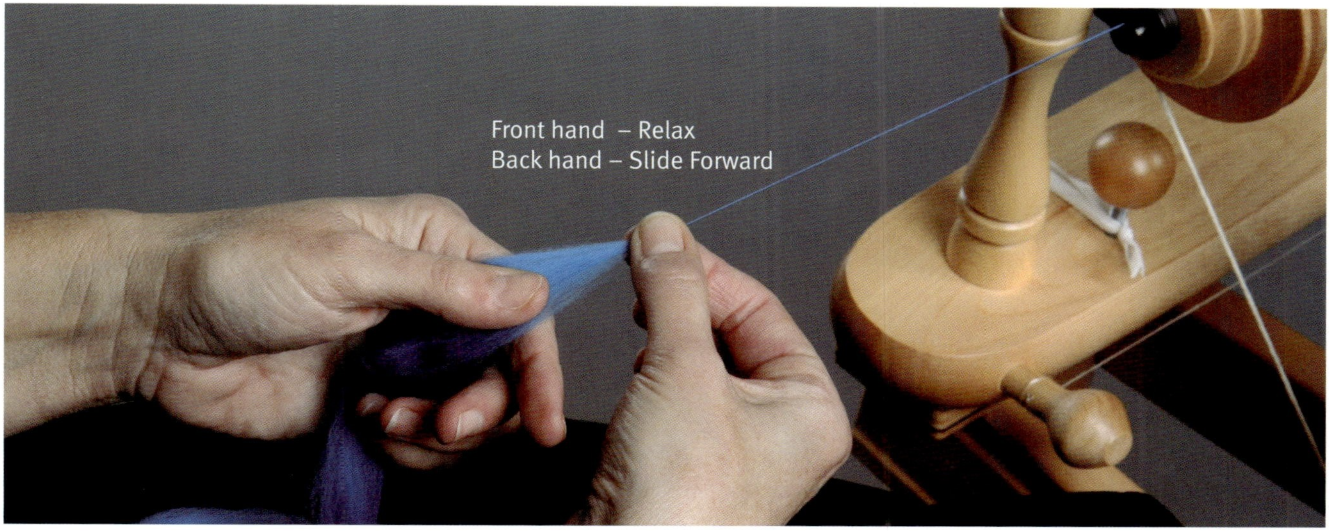

No pressure!

Release the pinch slightly on your front hand, letting the twist run along the drafted fibres but not into the drafting zone.

Keeping your front hand stationary, bring your back hand forward towards your front hand. Let the spun yarn slide through the thumb and index finger of your front hand and wind onto the bobbin. Your hands should be about 5cm (2ins) apart.

Now repeat the process.

Say the words to yourself if it helps to keep the rhythm going.

Front Hand	Pinch
Back Hand	Draft back
Front Hand	Relax
Back Hand	Slide forward

Your first efforts at spinning may not feel very relaxing as the biggest hurdle will be to keep the twist out of the drafting zone. Do not worry too much about it in the early stages of learning. Keep trying as it won't be long before your hand movements become quicker.

Remember to treadle slowly and steadily and keep the front hand still while the back moves backwards and forwards.

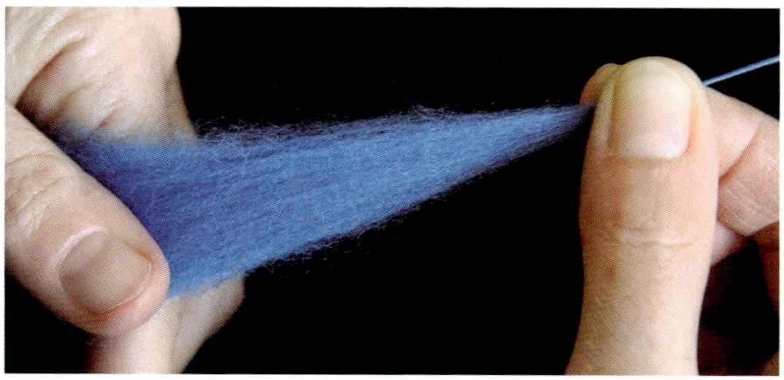

Correct spinning – the fibre between the orifice and front hand is twisted and there is no twist in the drafting zone

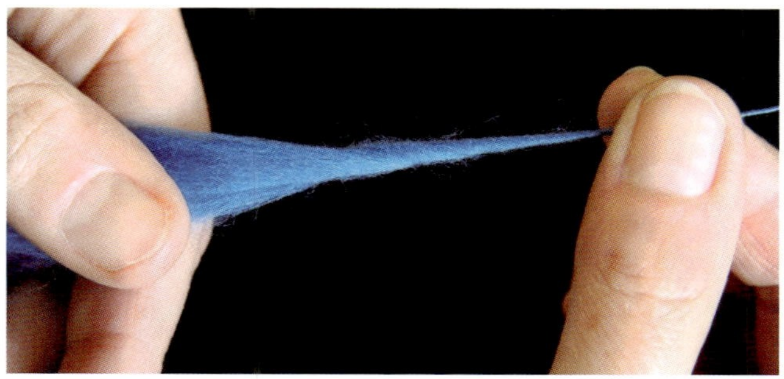

Incorrect – there is twist in the drafting zone

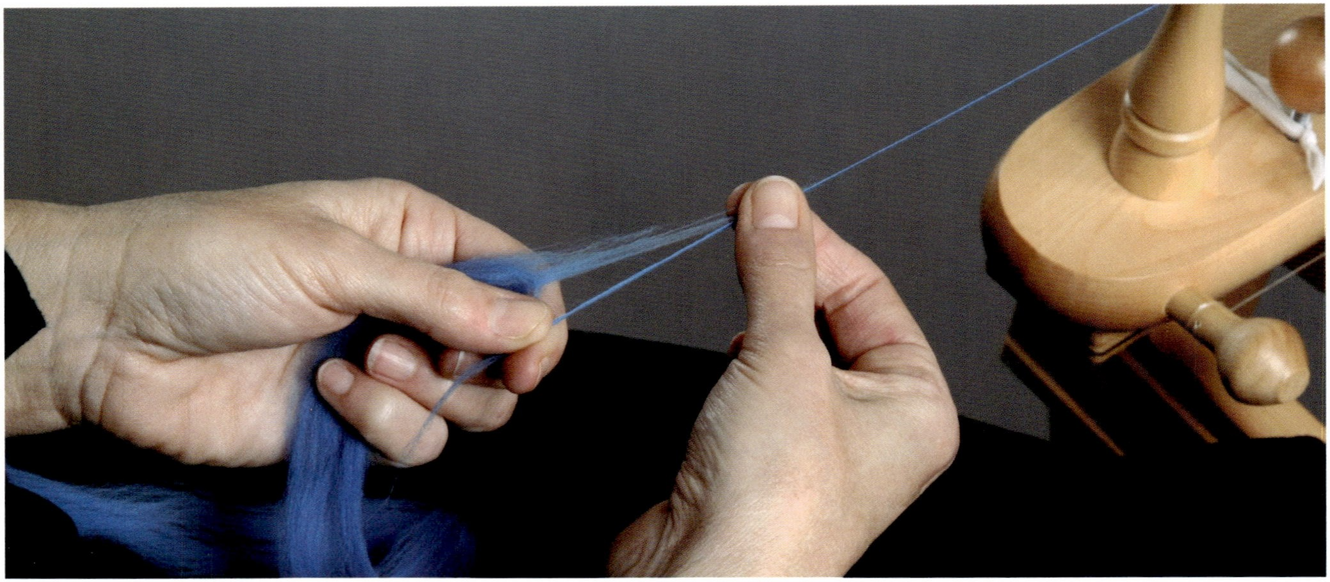

Joining in more fibre

Loosen a few fibres from the end of the staple or sliver and overlap with your spun yarn. Pinch off the twist with your front hand and start treadling. The new portion will catch onto your spun yarn and you can start the rhythm again.

Move the yarn along to the next hook on the flyer at regular intervals to fill the bobbin evenly.

As the bobbin fills, it becomes heavier and may require more tension for the yarn to be drawn in. Tighten it just a little at a time if you feel this happening.

How much twist?

Check the twist by pulling 15-20cm (6-8ins) off the bobbin and let it twist back on itself. It should look evenly plied with no twists or gaps. This will give you an estimate of the thickness of the finished yarn when plied.

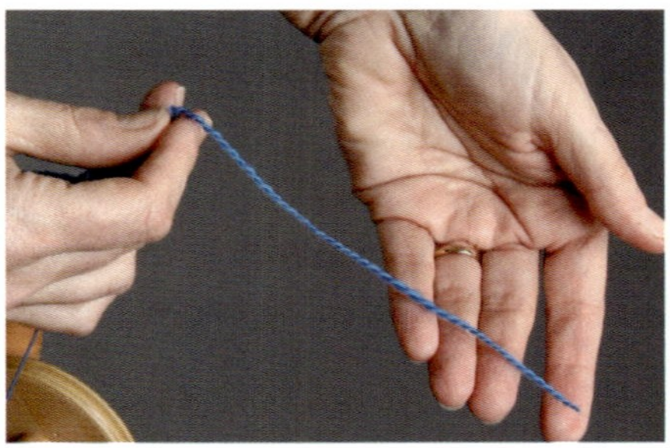

Evenly plied

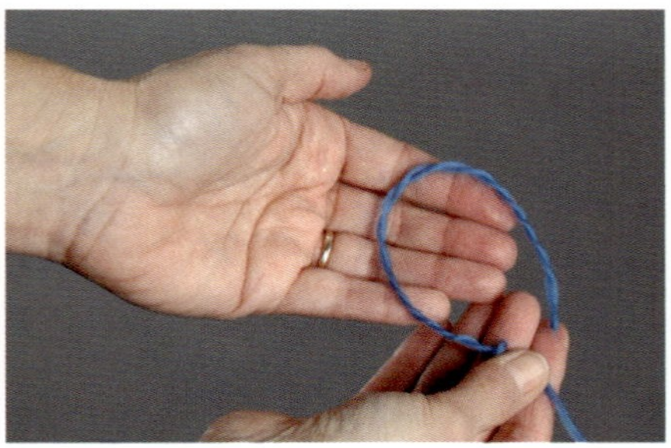

Not enough twist – add a little more next time by treadling faster or drafting slower

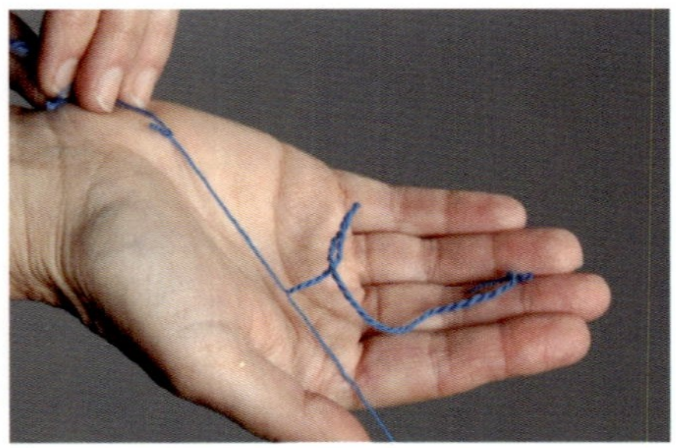

Too much twist – either slow down your treadling or speed up your hand movements a little

Hints and tips

The twist enters the drafting zone too soon: Keep your fingers pinched so the twist does not run into the drafting zone. Reduce the brake band tension.

The yarn does not wind onto the bobbin: There is little or no tension. Tighten the brake band tension in small amounts until you feel the yarn just pulling on. Check the yarn is not caught on any of the hooks.

The yarn twists back on itself between your hands and the orifice: There is not enough tension. Tighten the brake band tension in small amounts until you feel the yarn just pulling on.

The yarn keeps breaking: Relax your back hand to allow more fibres into the drafting zone or more twist may be needed. Try using a smaller whorl or treadling a little faster.

The yarn is too thick: Pinch firmly with your front hand and draft back further with your back hand.

The yarn is hard and stringy: There is too much twist. Try spinning with a larger whorl or treadling a little slower.

Plying – Making a two-ply yarn

The bobbins of spun singles need to be supported on a bobbin holder or lazy kate.

The spinning lesson on the previous page used a Z twist for the singles so you will be plying S twist, or anti-clockwise. If the singles are plied in the same direction as spinning, you will just be adding more twist and the yarn will be hard, over-twisted and kink back on itself.

Lazy kate

Competition lazy kate with tension system

Two singles separated ready for plying

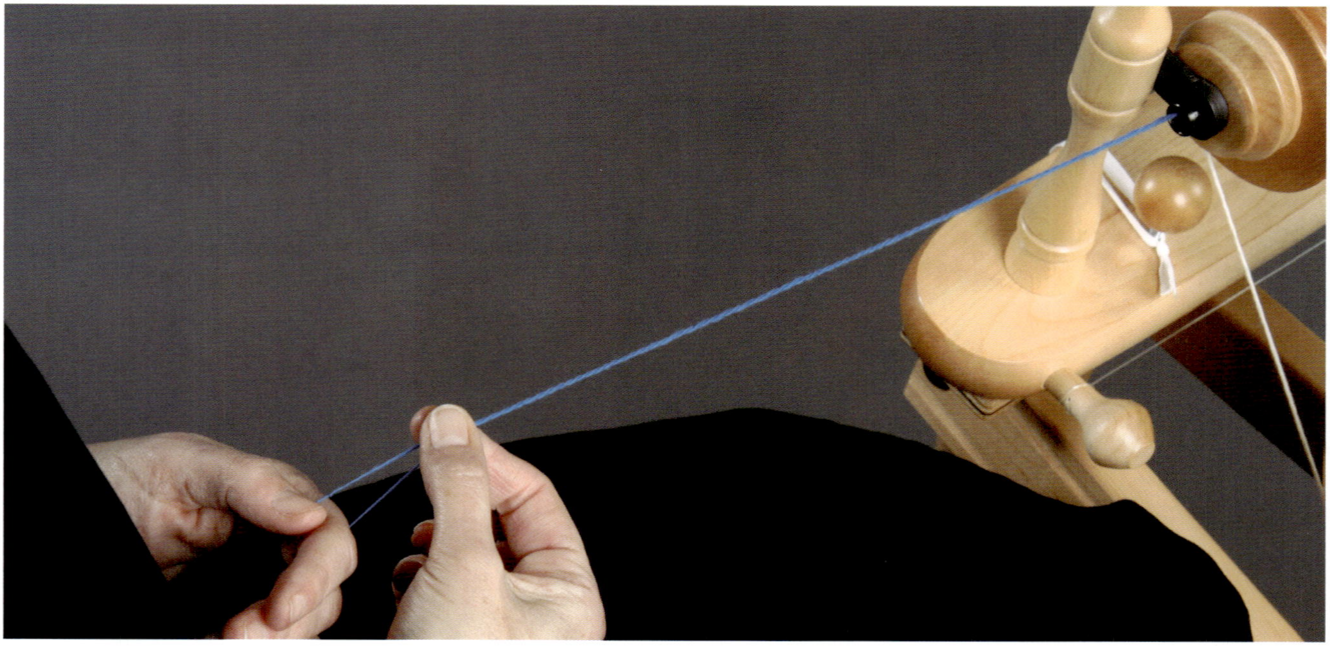

The two singles twisted together ready for feeding onto the bobbin

Tie a leader onto an empty bobbin and place it on the flyer shaft, threading the leader through the orifice, leaving about 20-25cm (8-10ins) hanging out as you did for the singles. Check the tension.

For easy, smooth plying, the lazy kate is best placed behind you. Make a loop at the end of the leader. Take the ends of the two singles through the loop and fold back on themselves for about 5cm (2ins). Pinch the folded ends lightly with your front hand.

With your back hand, use one finger to separate the threads. Position this hand close to your body in line with the orifice, keeping the singles taut.

Begin treadling anticlockwise. The twist will run down the length of the two singles. Keeping your back hand stationary, slide your front hand along the plied yarn until your two hands meet then pinch and feed the yarn into the orifice. It will take 4-6 treadles for the twist to accumulate along the length of the singles.

Now repeat the process:

Slide your front hand along the plied yarn

Pinch and feed into the orifice

The bobbin will fill up quickly so be sure to move your yarn at regular intervals to the next hook on the flyer.

As with your singles, the bobbin will get heavier as it fills up and you may need to increase the tension a little at a time to keep the yarn pulling on.

Judging the amount of twist

Your eyes are by far the best judge. When your two hands meet, stop treadling and take a close look at the yarn.

Check for a balanced yarn by letting it hang between the orifice and your hands. It should not twist in either direction.

If it looks loose and there are gaps between the two singles, it will need a little more twist – one or two more treadles as your front hand slides along.

If it looks hard and perhaps kinks back on itself, you need less twist – one or two less treadles.

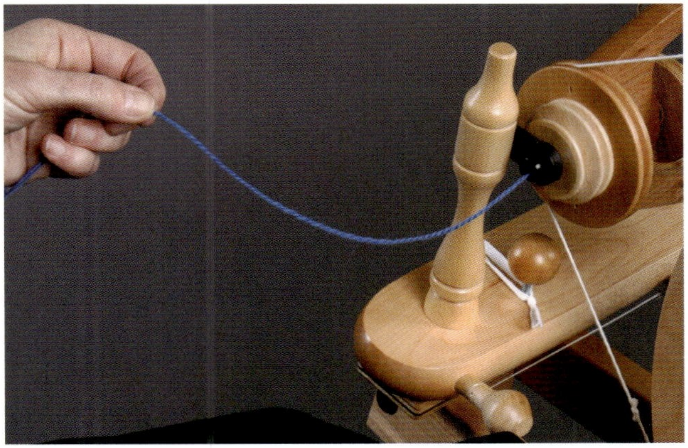

A balanced yarn

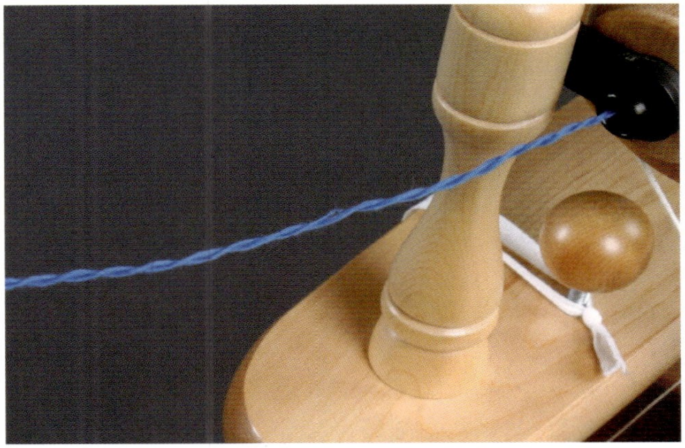

Underplied

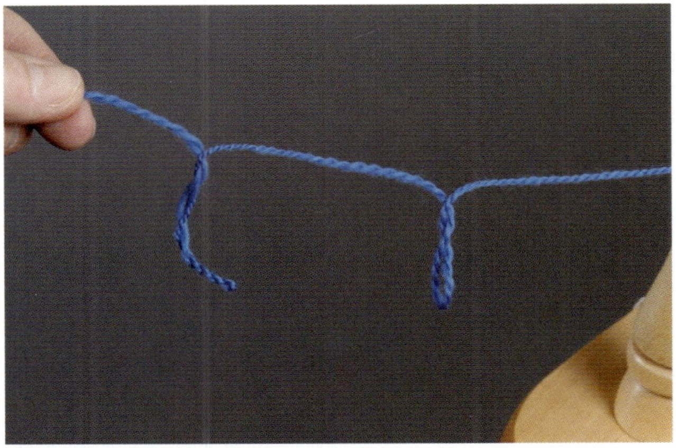

Overplied

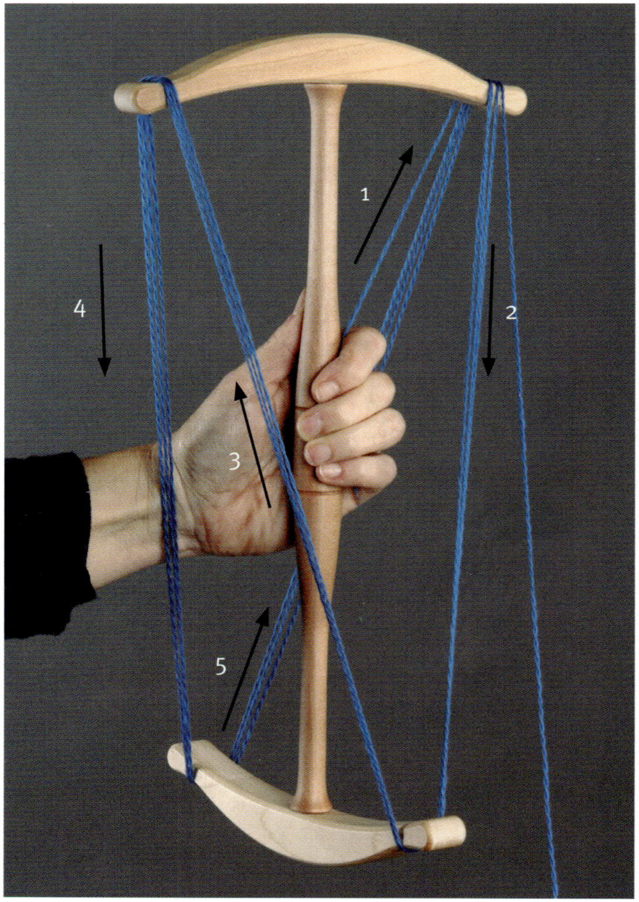

Winding the yarn around a niddy noddy

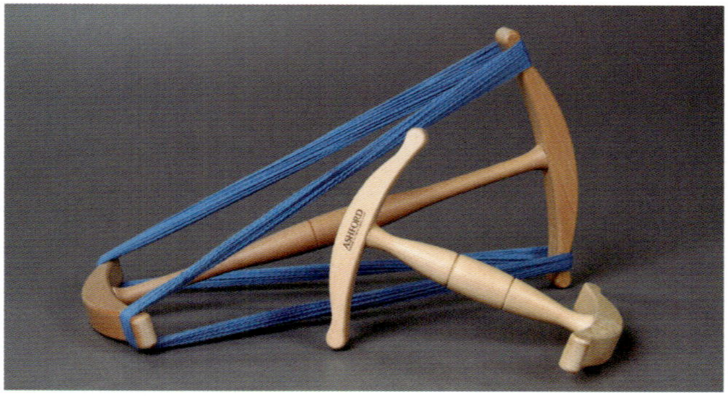

Niddy Noddy – for larger skeins
Sampler Niddy Noddy – ideal for samples and small skeins

Skeining

When the bobbin is full, your yarn needs to be skeined, or wound into a hank, and washed to set the twist. Most spinners use a niddy noddy for skeining.

Loosen off most of the tension on the bobbin. Hold the end of the yarn with the hand holding the niddy noddy, winding it around as shown in the photograph. Tie it off in several places, four should be enough. Remove the skein from the niddy noddy.

A balanced yarn

Balanced yarn

Let the skein hang loose with one hand. If it hangs straight, you have a balanced yarn.

Under-plied: The skein will twist in the same direction as plying, in this case S twist, to try and ply itself some more. Treadle a little faster next time, adding two or three more treadles before feeding the yarn onto the bobbin.

Over-plied: The skein will try and un-ply itself by twisting in the opposite direction to plying, in this case Z twist. Treadle slower next time, reducing the number of treadles by two or three.

Note: Sometimes freshly plied skeins may twist just a little when removed from the niddy noddy. This is nothing to worry about as the washing process will set the twist. It is only when the skein twists many times in either direction that a correction to the plying would be needed.

Washing your beautiful handspun yarn

If you chose to spin with greasy wool, use the washing method on page 52. If your wool is clean, just a light wash is needed to set the twist. I like to use a bucket of warm water and a liquid wool wash. Soak the yarn for about an hour then rinse in the same water temperature. Wrap in a towel and remove excess water by either rolling up the towel and squeezing tightly or using the spin cycle on your washing machine.

Navajo plying – making a three-ply yarn

Navajo plying is making a three-ply yarn from one single. This is a great way of creating a colourful yarn and perfect for preserving the colour order in multi-coloured slivers. Navajo plying makes a strong yarn which is excellent for sock knitting. It is an economical method of plying as all the single is used.

Multi-coloured single ready for navajo plying

The single on this bobbin was spun with a small amount of each colour in the same order using a small whorl. More twist is needed in the single to allow for the fact that twist will be removed from three singles as you ply, instead of the usual two.

It is easy to over-ply so set your wheel to its largest whorl and treadle very slowly. Use your back hand to draw the single through the loop, presenting three strands for plying. The front hand will smooth the plied yarn and feed onto the bobbin.

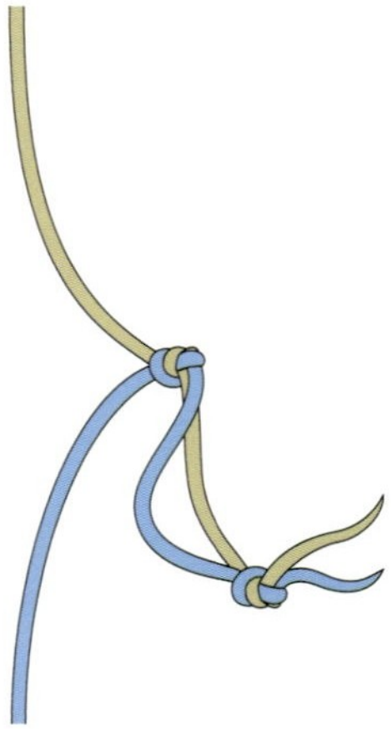

1. Tie the single onto the leader. Make another knot approximately 15cm (6ins) away from the first knot.

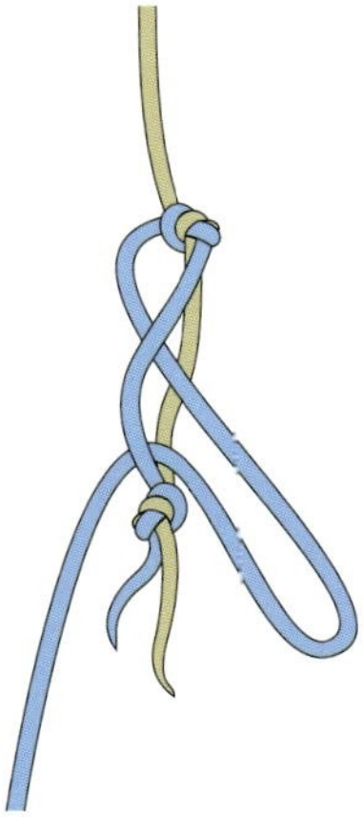

2. Hold the loop open with your back hand, using whichever fingers feel comfortable. Draw the single through the loop for about 30cm (12ins) with your forefinger.

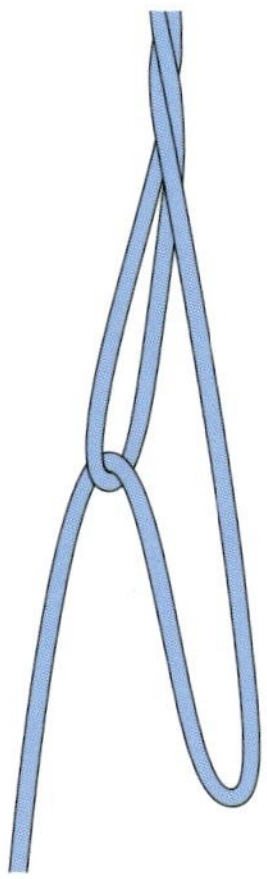

3. Begin treadling S twist and count the number of treadles until the three strands are twisted into a nice, rounded looking yarn. This will usually be 4 or 5 treadles.

4. Feed the plied yarn onto the bobbin with the front hand. Draw the yarn through the loop again, count the treadles and feed the plied yarn onto the bobbin. After a while, the two actions will become simultaneous and you will settle into a smooth rhythm.

Drawing the single through the loop

The plied yarn ready to feed onto the bobbin

Once the initial challenges of learning to spin have been overcome, you will soon develop the freedom to create the perfect yarn for your project. Designing yarn is really just planning and making decisions. Thickness, twist, colour, texture, lustre and durability are all choices to be made. Hand spun yarn can be smooth, even and naturally coloured, or bright, fuzzy and fabulously textured, and everything in between.

Any fibre can be spun into a thread but most are enhanced by a harmonious blend of fibre, carding technique and spinning style. In this section you will learn about the spinning methods to create worsted, semi-worsted and woollen yarns. Different carding techniques are used to prepare fibre for the various spinning styles and these are described beginning on page 34.

Drive ratio

Different fibres need different amounts of twist to best show off their unique characteristics. You can achieve this by adjusting your treadling speed to add more or less twist, but it can also be done by altering the drive ratio on your spinning wheel.

Whilst not vitally important in the early stages of learning to spin, as you become more experienced, it will be very useful to understand what drive ratio means and how it affects your yarn.

Each of the Ashford range of spinning wheels has a choice of drive ratios, which can be altered by moving the drive band to a different groove in the flyer whorl. On some models, the tension on the drive band will need to be adjusted accordingly.

How it works

The faster the flyer turns compared to the drive wheel, the more twist there will be in the yarn. For each revolution of the drive wheel, the flyer will turn 'x' number of times. For example, when the Ashford Traditional Scotch tension wheel is set to the largest whorl, the flyer will turn 6.5 times for each revolution of the drive wheel, or 6.5:1. This is the slowest speed for the wheel and will put the least amount of twist into the yarn. The fastest speed on this wheel is 17.5:1, almost three times faster than the slowest speed. This will introduce much more twist into the yarn.

As a general rule, fine, short fibres, such as Merino wool or angora, need plenty of twist to hold them together whereas longer, coarser fibres need less twist. Having a choice of drive ratios means you can treadle at the same speed for varying amounts of twist in the yarn. If your spinning wheel has just one drive ratio, you will need to adjust the treadling speed to suit the amount of twist required.

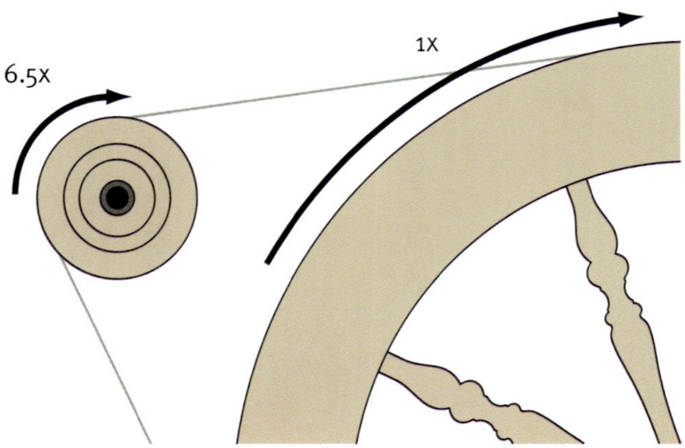

Largest whorl = slowest speed = less twist

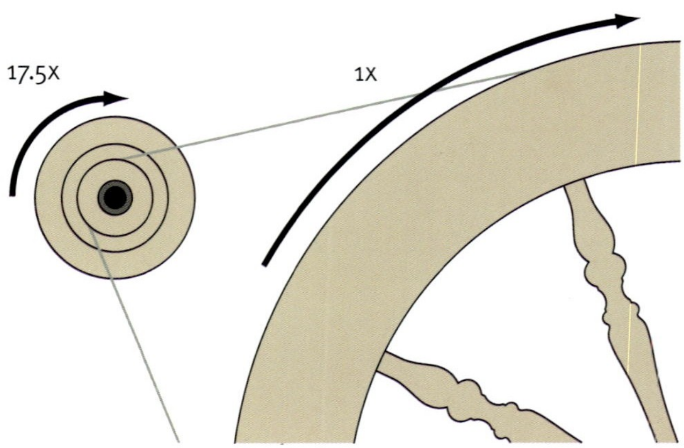

Smallest whorl = fastest speed = more twist

Twists per inch

The amount of twist in a yarn will reveal much about its style. A lightly twisted yarn will contain a lot of air and be soft and fuzzy and have good elasticity, whereas a highly twisted yarn will be smoother, heavier and less elastic. Each style of yarn is suited to different end products.

The rhythmical nature of spinning means that most of the time there will be a consistent amount of twist in the yarn. But what if you prefer to be in control of the amount of twist, want to recreate a yarn at will or describe it to others? You can do this by measuring the number of twists per inch.

As you have learned, the drive ratio on your wheel controls the amount of twist going into the yarn. So far I have only talked about 'more' or 'less' twist but you can use the drive ratio information in a more meaningful way.

For example, when the drive ratio on a wheel is set at 6:1, this means that if you draft 1 inch (2.5cm) of fibre and let the wheel turn for one revolution, there will be 6 twists in that 1 inch (2.5cm) of fibre. If you consistently draft and treadle this way you will control the amount of twist throughout your entire project.

If you draft that same inch of fibre and let the wheel turn twice, there will be 12 twists per inch.

Once you have settled on the amount of twist you need for a project, pull a length from the bobbin and let it ply back on itself. Cut this off and attach it to a piece of card, noting the twists per inch for future reference.

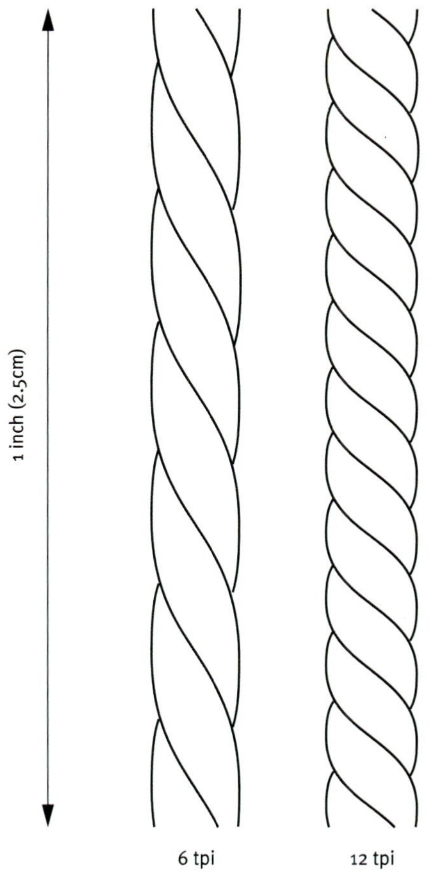

Worsted spun yarn

Worsted yarn

A worsted yarn is smooth and strong with no air trapped around the fibres.

Worsted yarns are best suited to hard-wearing outer garments, rugs, blankets and weaving warps and are perfect to reflect light and show off the natural sheen of wool fleeces such as Corriedale or English Leicester, and other fibres such as silk and Tencel. There is good stitch definition in knitting.

When spinning fleece, it is spun from the butt end (the cut end during shearing) of long stapled fibres that have been combed or flick carded to keep them parallel and remove any short fibres.

Spinning from the butt end smooths down the overlapping scales on the fibres. Store the carded staples with the butt ends facing one way and the tips facing the other for ease of spinning. If you are a beginner, you may not easily recognise which end is which so make a note on the box.

Cut end

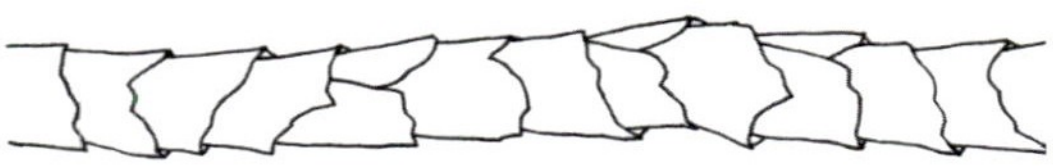

Wool fibre magnified

Commercially prepared combed top is ideal for worsted spinning as the combing process has aligned the fibres for you.

The short forward and short backward draft both produce a worsted yarn. In both methods the twist never enters the drafting zone.

Short backward draft

As described on page 18 the back hand holds the fibre, drafts back and slides forward to feed the spun yarn onto the bobbin. The front hand remains stationary and controls the twist by pinching and relaxing. The front hand smooths down any loose fibres, not lifting from the yarn while spinning.

Short forward draft

This method is the reverse of the short backward draft. The back hand holds the fibre and remains stationary while the front hand drafts the fibre forward and slides back smoothing the fibres that have been twisted.

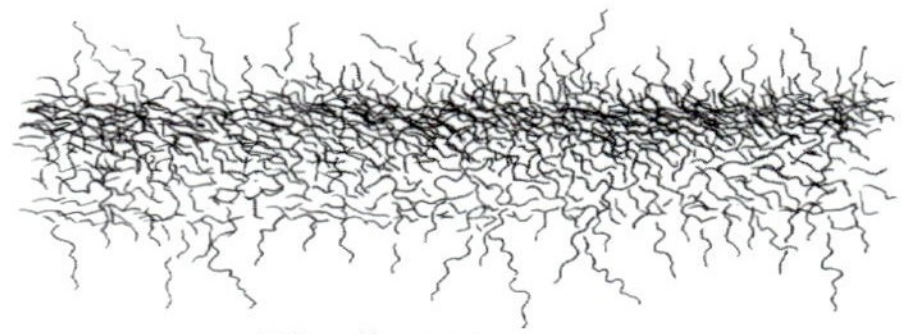

Woollen spun yarn

Woollen yarn

A woollen yarn allows the fibres to wrap around each other to trap air, resulting in a soft and bouncy yarn. It is suitable for lightweight knits, blankets, coats and jackets. A woollen yarn will 'full' when it is washed, making it stronger. In hand woven woollen textiles, the gaps between the threads are filled in during washing.

The long draw method of spinning produces a woollen yarn which is usually spun from short stapled fibres that have been arranged randomly in hand carded rolags or drum carded batts.

Another method is to fold a small piece of sliver over your forefinger and spin from the fold.

Long draw

This is the traditional drafting method for a woollen yarn. It is a rapid method of spinning and one well worth learning for spinning other fibres such as mohair and cotton. In woollen spinning, the twist is allowed to enter the drafting zone.

Both hands wait at the orifice for the twist to accumulate, about 5 treadles. The back hand drafts the fibre out to an arm's length at right angles to the orifice, while at the same time, the front hand remains stationary near the orifice and controls the twist by quickly pinching and relaxing to let in enough twist to strengthen the yarn. The front hand releases the pinch and the back hand quickly feeds the spun yarn onto the bobbin.

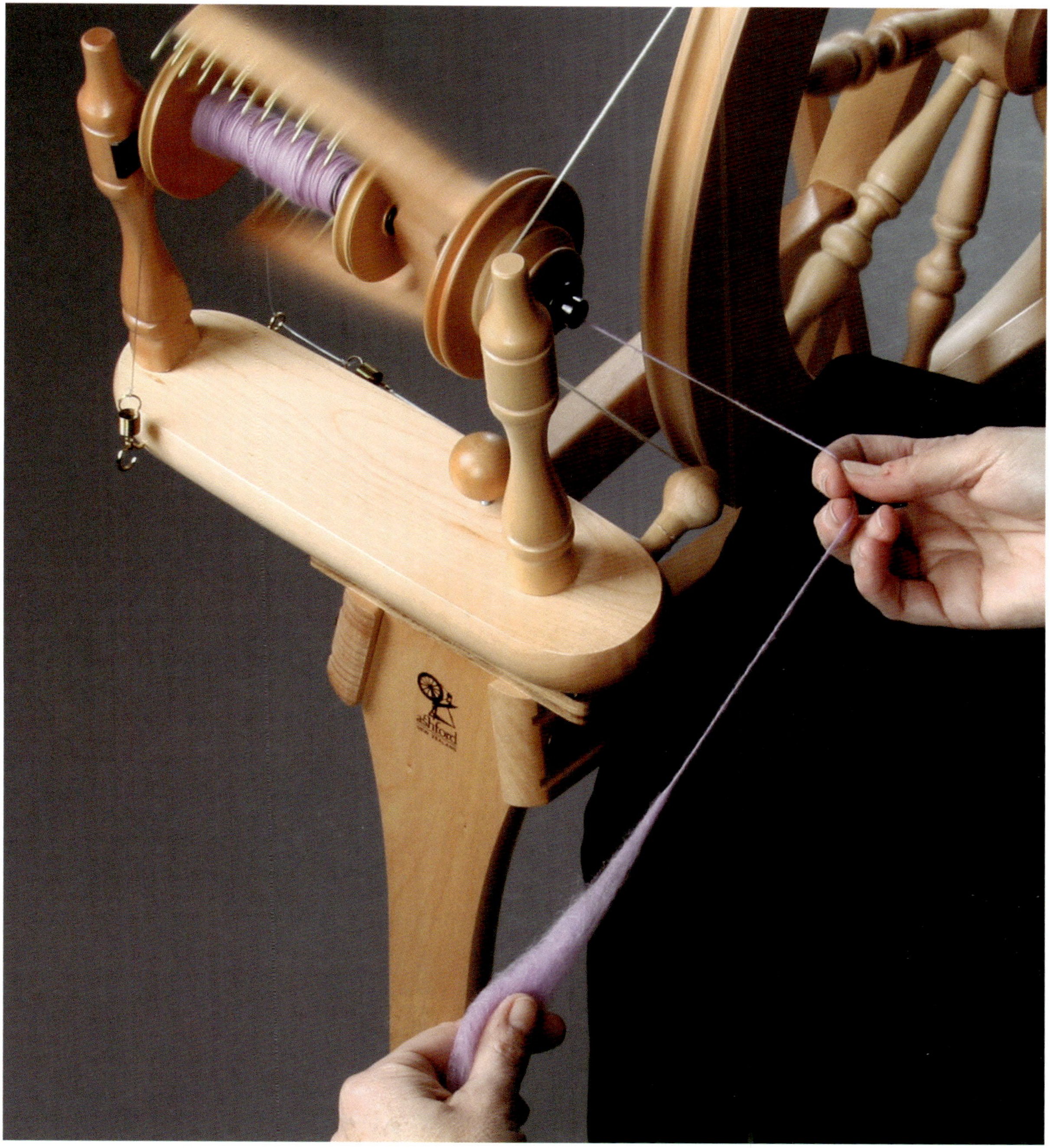

Spinning the long draw

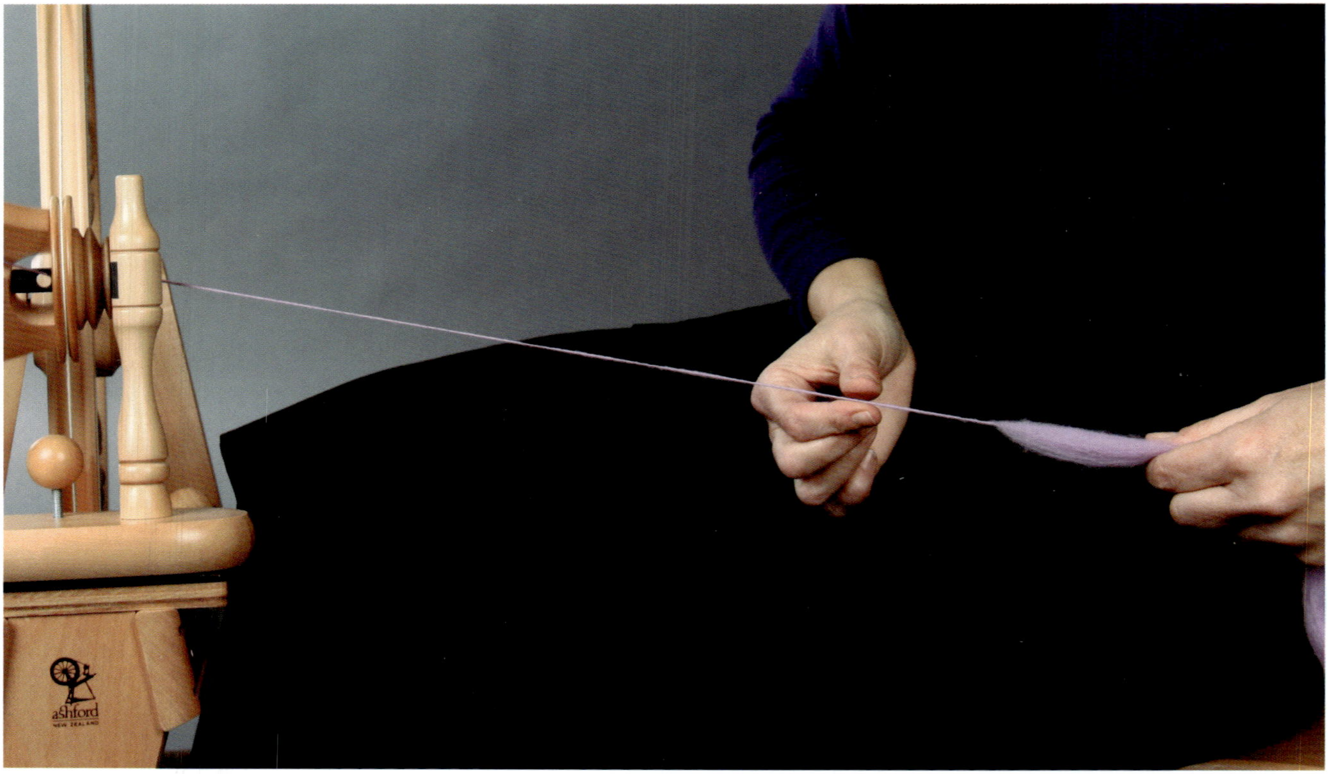

Spinning the medium draft

Semi-worsted yarn

A semi-worsted yarn is somewhere between woollen and worsted. It is spun using the medium draft which follows naturally from the short forward or backward draft. As there is no smoothing of the twisted fibres as with worsted spinning, this method produces a light, airy yarn.

The fibre needs to be well carded so it can flow freely from the back hand. Use hand carded rolags or drum carded batts.

Medium draft

This is a lovely relaxed, quicker method of drafting that allows the spinner greater control over the yarn thickness and twist. There is both spun and unspun fibre between the two hands and a long length of spun yarn is visible making it easier to achieve a constant thickness in the yarn.

The back hand holds the fibre and drafts back in one smooth action as far as is comfortable (about the hip). The front hand 'supports' but does not pinch the spun yarn during drafting and can either remain stationary near the orifice or follow the back hand at a constant distance. Then both hands move toward the orifice to feed the yarn onto the bobbin.

Fine spinning

A fine yarn has more than 18 wraps per inch. Fine fibres such as Merino wool, alpaca or silk need more twist to hold them together. Select the smallest groove on the flyer whorl. If your wheel has one groove, you will need to treadle faster than usual to introduce the extra twist required. Spin with a very light tension. Start spinning and further adjust the tension if necessary.

Spinning a fine yarn is really no different than spinning a medium thickness yarn. Everything is just on a smaller scale. Small hand movements and smaller amounts of fibre in your hands. For combed top, divide staple lengths into two or three portions for better control of the fibre.

I prefer the short forward or short backward draft for a fine worsted yarn, however, the long draw can also be used for a woollen yarn from short-stapled fibres.

Using your chosen drafting method, try spinning as fine as you possibly can, reducing the number of fibres in the drafting zone to just a few. Take your time and concentrate a little more than usual. Check the twist at regular intervals by pulling a length of yarn off the bobbin, letting it ply back on itself. It should look rounded and well plied, but not tight and stringy.

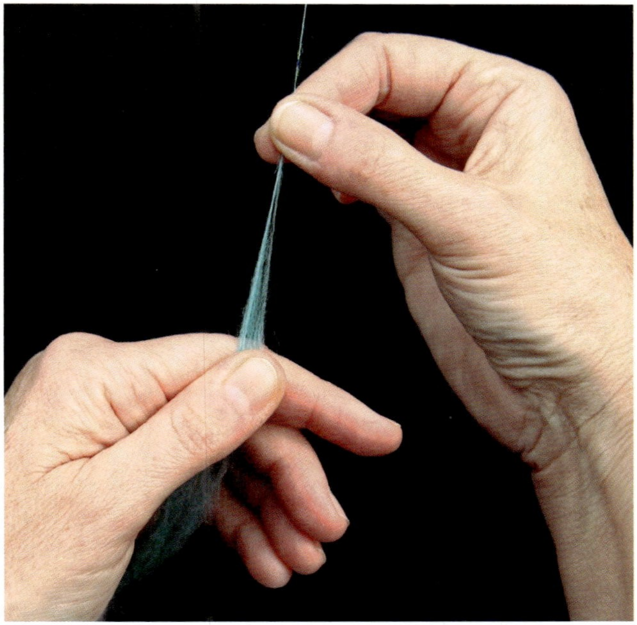

Spinning a fine yarn with a Merino/silk blend

Bulky spinning

Bulky yarns have less than 12 wraps per inch. Spinning bulky yarns is quick and fun. You can let yourself go and be expressive with colour, texture and different fibres. Making thick yarn is more or less the opposite to making fine yarn – quicker hand movements, larger amounts of fibre and relaxed spinning.

Set your flyer whorl to the largest groove as not much twist will be needed to hold the fibres together. Treadle a little slower than usual to prevent the larger number of fibres being overtwisted.

I like to use the short forward draft, holding the fibre loosely in my back hand, feeding the fibre into the orifice with short, quick movements.

Spinning a thick yarn with Corriedale

Although you can spin most fibres without any preparation, drafting is much easier and spinning more relaxing if the fibre is teased open by carding. Each carding method enables you to spin a different style of yarn. You have already read about woollen and worsted yarns and drafting techniques. Now you can blend that knowledge with carding methods to spin the most suitable yarn for a project.

Flick carding

A flick carder has several rows of metal teeth which open up fleece staples quickly and efficiently and aligns the fibres for worsted spinning.

You can flick card washed or unwashed fibre.

You will need a cloth or apron to protect your clothing and catch the dirt which will fall out as you are carding, even with washed wool. Some spinners like to use a piece of leather or vinyl. Short fibres in the staples will be removed as you card and collect between the teeth. Remove them at regular intervals to keep carding efficient.

Card a reasonable quantity of staples at one time to give you enough for a good spinning session.

Flick carder

Ready to card the tip of the staple

1. Hold the cut end of the staple firmly in one hand and with this hand resting on your knee, gently ‘bounce’ the carder up and down on the tips. Try not to drag the carder through the staple.

2. Turn the staple over and card the other side.

3. Now hold the carded end and flick the cut end of the staple in the same way.

The staple should be free of dirt and all fibres separated from each other

Hand carding

This method of carding produces a small rolag for woollen spinning. Hand carders are used in pairs to prepare several staples of fleece at one time. I prefer not to use my hand carders with greasy wool. The grease and dirt build-up makes them very difficult to clean. Spinners who spin mostly in the grease are often happy to dedicate a pair of carders for carding greasy wool.

Hand carders are great for colour and fibre blending using wool sliver and other fibres. Experiment with different blends – add lustre with silk, softness with Merino or alpaca or perhaps some coloured sliver with a natural fleece.

Set of hand carders

Filling the carder with staples of Romney fleece

1. With one of the carders on your knee, place teased staples of fibre on the teeth at the handle end to catch it onto the carder, drawing down gently towards the top end as you let go. It does not matter which way the tips face. Work your way across the carder filling it to the depth of the teeth. Over-filling the carder will make the fibre difficult to manage.

Brushing

2. Hold the carders as illustrated. Gently brush the fibre, at first just catching the ends of the staples, gradually increasing the overlap until the carders overlap completely. The teeth should not be meshing together. At this stage about half of the fibre will be on each carder.

Transferring the fibre onto the left carder

3. Position the left-hand carder in an upright position, still on your knee. With the teeth of the carders facing each other, place the top edge of the right-hand carder against the bottom edge of the left-hand carder. Make a swift movement up with the left carder which will now hold all the fibre.

Repeat the brushing process. Again, there will be about half the fibre on each carder.

Transferring the fibre onto the right carder

4. Now the underside of the batt needs to be carded. Change the grip of your hands as illustrated. Position the right-hand carder in an upright position on your knee and with the teeth of the carders facing each other, place the top edge of the left-hand carder against the bottom edge of the right-hand carder. Make a swift movement up with the right-hand carder, pulling all the fibre off the left carder. The right carder will now hold all the fibre. Brush again.

Getting ready to remove the carded batt

5. Hold both the carders as illustrated. Make a swift, light movement up with one carder, then a swift, light movement up with the other. All the fibre should now be sitting on the teeth of one carder.

Rolling the batt off the carder

6. Roll the fibre from the top edge towards the bottom to remove it from the carder.

Carded rolag ready for woollen spinning

Drum carder with two speeds

Drum carding

The drum carder is the ideal tool for preparing large amounts of fibre for spinning. You can use your carder to make beautiful, easy to spin batts using natural coloured fleece, or be creative with colour and fibre blends using commercially prepared sliver. Many colours can be processed in several ways for colour effects in your spinning. If you prefer to do your own dyeing, the drum carder is a great way to distribute the colour evenly through the batt.

It is important to use the appropriate carding cloth for the type of fibre you intend carding. The fine drum carder (72 pt) is suitable for most of your carding needs, however the coarse carder (36 pt) is designed for stronger fibres such as Lincoln or English Leicester.

If you have a two-speed drum carder, use the slower ratio (6:1) for thorough carding of fleece staples and gentle carding of luxury fibres. The faster ratio (4:1) is suitable for colour blending of sliver, or recarding.

The carder is clamped to the table when in use to prevent it from sliding around. This frees up both hands and allows you to do the job efficiently. Before using the carder, check that both drums are free of all fibre. This is particularly important when changing from one colour to another.

All fibre needs to be opened up before you feed it onto the carder. You should be able to see the infeed tray through the teased fibre.

Feed the fibre on like this

Not like this

Fleece

It will be kinder on your machine to card fleece that is clean, free of vegetation and well teased. It will not remove dirt, thistles, short cuts, or lumps – it will only distribute them through the entire batt. It is no fun to be picking them out as you are spinning. When carding fleece I like to give the tips of the staples a quick flick with the flick carder and then tease the other fibres open with my fingers.

Place your well-teased fibre onto the infeed tray and turn the handle slowly and steadily. Feed the fibre in as you turn the handle in a clockwise direction. Keep the fibre between the guides, away from the edges of the drum, to avoid it being drawn around the axles.

Do not hold onto the fibre as you feed it in.

There should be little or no fibre accumulating on the small drum. If there is, reduce the amount of fibre on the infeed tray and turn the handle more slowly.

If some fibres do get caught on the small drum, stop carding when the seam of the carding cloth on the small drum is showing and slide your awl under the fibre along the metal strip. Lift the fibres up and onto the big drum. Continue carding.

Fill the drum to about the depth of the teeth. If fibre starts collecting on the small drum, it is usually an indication the main drum is full.

Separating the fibre along the doffing strip

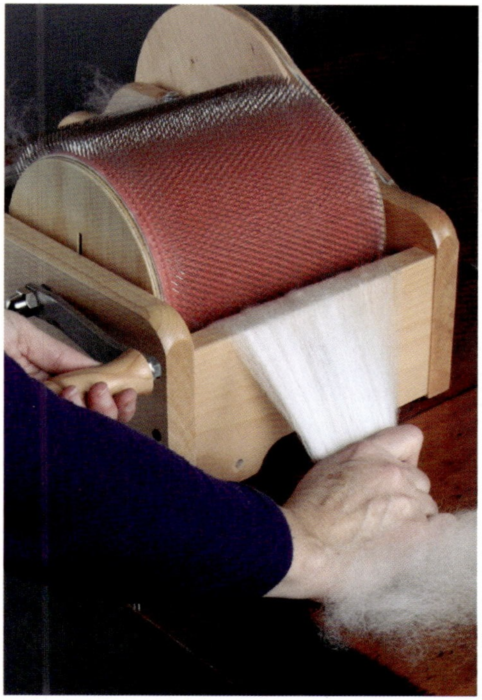

Peeling the batt off the drum

Removing the batt

Position the doffing strip of the large drum so it is on top. Slide the doffer (sometimes called an awl) under the fibre about half way along the metal strip and gently lift the fibres up until they separate. Continue along the remaining half. Make sure the batt is separated all the way across otherwise it won't peel cleanly off the drum.

Now gather up the ends of the fibre and pull down over the back beam with a small amount of tension. The drum will turn freely in the opposite direction to carding and the batt should peel away cleanly from the carding cloth.

Divide the batt in half down its length. Draw each half out lengthwise then spread out to the width of the infeed tray and card each piece again. Remove the batt and hold it up to the light. If the fibres look evenly distributed and there are no clumpy looking areas, then it is done. Otherwise, divide it in two and pass it through the carder again.

Splitting the batt in half lengthwise

Stretching the batt into a sliver

Rolling the batt widthwise for worsted or semi-worsted spinning

Preparing your batt for spinning

For semi-worsted spinning, the batt is pulled lengthwise into a sliver and spun from the end. Roll it up widthwise, then holding it firmly with your hands about 25-30cm (10-12ins) apart, gently pull until the fibres start to stretch. If you pull too hard it will drift apart.

Move one hand to where the fibre moved and the other about the same distance apart as they were before and pull again. Work your way up and down the sliver until it is as thin as you prefer for spinning. If the fibre won't move easily when you start pulling, place your hands further apart.

To spin a woollen yarn, create rolags by dividing the batt into shorter lengths and rolling them as shown in the diagram. Spinning from the end of the rolags effectively means the fibres are being drafted from a random arrangement instead of parallel as for worsted spinning.

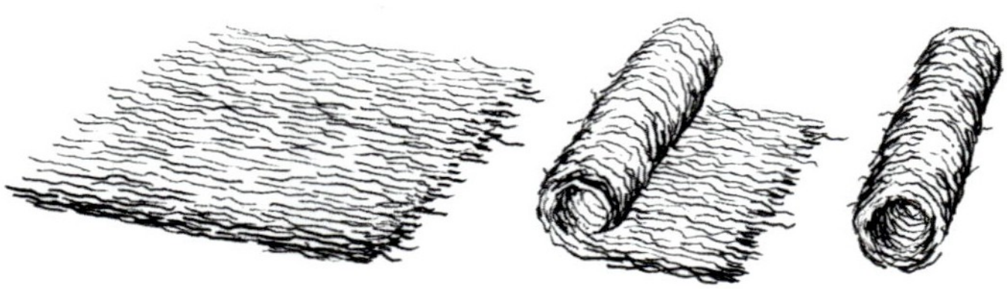

Sliver ready for semi-worsted spinning

Rolags ready for woollen spinning

Blending colours side-by-side

Colour blending with sliver

Commercial slivers are usually wound fairly firmly into "bumps" after carding and can become compacted. They are usually too thick to feed directly onto the carder and may put a strain on your machine and possibly tear the fibres.

Peel a strip off the side of the sliver to open up the fibres and give you a manageable amount to work with. Gently pull on the strip to lengthen it a little, but not so much that it drifts apart, and spread it out widthwise a little.

Fibre can be arranged in several ways on the drum carder to achieve different effects with colour in your spinning. Use washed and dyed staples or commercial sliver. If you are using dyed fleece, card each colour separately before you begin blending. In this section I have used coloured slivers from the Ashford Corriedale range.

Blending colours side-by-side

This technique makes a multi-coloured sliver. Take a 30cm (12ins) length of sliver and peel a thin strip off the side. Draw it out a little lengthwise and feed each colour separately onto the carder, placing them side by side. The wider each strip of colour, the brighter and clearer it will be in the finished yarn.

One pass

Two passes

Blending colours in layers

This technique makes a heathered or flecked yarn or a completely new colour. Be careful with this method that you don't overblend and end up with dull colours. Keep in mind that the spinning and plying process will blend the colours a little more. For best results, use three or four colours.

Peel off a section of your sliver, spread it out widthwise and feed onto the carder, filling the width of the drum. Repeat with each colour. After the first pass, divide the batt in half lengthwise, spread each half out to the width of the drum and card again. Keep dividing the batt and carding until the colours are blended to your liking.

Three passes

Ashford Merino sliver passed through the carder three times
Grape Jelly, Lagoon and Bean Sprout

Laying out silk on a carded Merino batt

Fibre blending

Fibre blending on the drum carder is exciting and fun. Stunning yarns can be spun from blends of luxurious fibres. Imagine wearing a woven or knitted scarf spun from a blend of Merino wool, silk and angora! The drape would be superb.

Put some thought into the qualities you would like to come through in your project. Silk and Suri alpaca will give lustre. Fine wools, alpaca and angora will add softness. Angora and Samoyed dog will give fluffiness.

Most luxury fibres cannot be carded easily on their own and will collect on the small drum. This is because they are either too short, or too fine. You can successfully card "luxury" fibres by blending them with longer fibres of wool. Instead of being caught on the small drum, the short, fine fibres are assisted onto the big drum by the wool fibres. Fitting a packer brush will also minimise build-up on the small drum. It helps control fine fibres such as angora, alpaca, mohair and silk and allows a thicker batt to be made.

For a thorough blend, card the wool separately before adding other fibres.

Folding the batt to encase the silk

Packer brush accessory on the drum carder

1. Spread the wool batt out lengthwise a little and then widthwise until it is about twice the width of the carder. Tease open the luxury fibre and spread it evenly over half the width of the wool batt.

2. Fold the remaining half of the batt over onto the luxury fibre, encasing it between two layers of wool. Feed the folded batt onto the carder, turning the handle very slowly and steadily. If the fibre supply buckles, it is too thick. Stop turning the drum, pull out the batt a little then continue carding. Do not hold onto the fibre as it goes into the carder.

3. Remove the batt and divide it in half lengthwise. Spread each half out to the width of the drum and card again. Blending different fibres takes a little more work than blending colours and you may need to make 3 or 4 passes for a thorough blend.

The proportion of each fibre you use in a blend will affect the appearance and handle of the final yarn. It only takes small amount of angora, as little as 10%, for its softness to be felt.

When adding silk, you will need at least 20% in a blend to show off its lustrous quality.

Luxury fibres are more expensive than wool so take some time to carefully plan your project and think about what qualities you want in your final yarn.

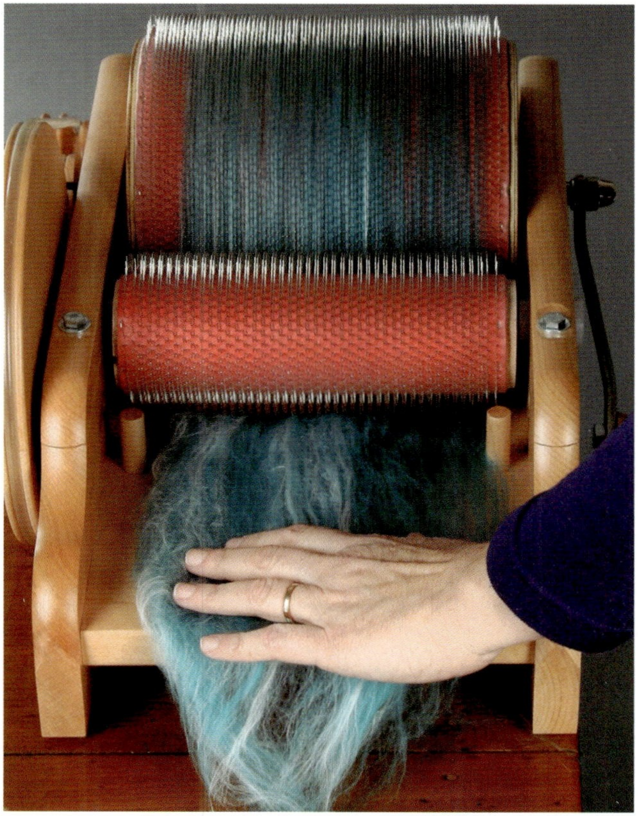

Carding the blend a second time

Fibre for spinning

One of the joys of hand spinning is the fantastic variety of fibre available to spin, most of it conveniently washed and carded, or combed, in an array of natural and dyed colours ready for spinning.

While wool will always be a favourite, fibres such as Suri alpaca, Tencel and bamboo are gaining in popularity. Spinners are thriving on exploring them and enjoying the opportunity to try something new. Once you are comfortable with spinning wool, I have no doubt you will be curious about them too. In this section there is information on a variety of animal (protein) and vegetable (cellulose) fibres. Some are more challenging to spin than others. Do try as many as you can as your spinning skills will develop rapidly, giving you the confidence to match your spinning technique to the fibre you are working with.

All of these fibres look beautiful in their own right but often they can be enhanced by blending with each other. Don't be afraid to experiment by either hand or drum carding or perhaps plying two different singles for unusual effects.

Wool

Wool is the fibre most spinners choose to start with because it is easy to spin. Unlike the smooth, slippery fibres of silk or angora, each wool fibre has an outer layer of overlapping scales which helps it cling to its neighbour during drafting. In addition, the natural lubricant of grease in wool helps the fibres to draft more easily.

Fleece wool grows in locks or bundles called staples which vary in length between breeds. For your first spinning experience, I recommend a staple length of 10-12cm (4-5ins). Much shorter and longer staples can be spun of course, but these will require some spinning experience. The staples have a regular wave pattern from end to end called crimp. The finer the wool, the closer the crimp spacing.

Sheep's wool is a truly wonderful fibre. Its versatility and many qualities make it a very popular choice with spinners. It can be blended with other fibres such as silk, angora, mohair or alpaca, to create gorgeous luxury yarns, and it takes dye beautifully. Its elasticity makes it durable and wrinkle resistant, and it can stretch up to 30 percent beyond its normal length and return to its original size.

There is a breed for every purpose in a range of wonderful natural colours from white to rich, dark brown. Sheep that have fibres with any colour other than white are known as 'black and coloured'.

Before you begin your fibre preparation, you will need to decide whether to spin with washed or unwashed (greasy) staples. Card and spin a few staples of both to find out which you prefer and read the information on page 52 to help you make a choice.

Corriedale skein

Selecting a fleece

The quality and beauty of handspun yarn depends very much on the quality of the wool from the sheep. There are many breeds of sheep suitable for spinning but not all breeds are suited for all purposes. Spinners often find it irresistible to buy a fleece which either just looks fantastic or they love the colour. Do put some thought into what you might do with that fleece. Much of your time will be invested in preparing and spinning your wool therefore you would be wise to choose an appropriate fleece for the intended project.

For example, a Merino fleece will have very fine fibres that will spin a beautiful soft, fine yarn. This would not be a good choice if your garment needs to be hard-wearing. The Merino would be ideal for a garment to be worn next to the skin – perhaps a scarf, lacy shawl or baby wear.

Corriedale staples

What to look for in a fleece

When buying your first fleece, take a really good look at it. If space permits, remove it from the bag so you can examine the whole fleece for any faults that might be present. Here are some qualities to look for:

Staple: The crimp should be evenly spaced along the length of the staple through the whole fleece.

Cleanliness: All fleeces have a certain amount of dirt and dust in them. Avoid fleeces that appear excessively dirty or have a large amount of vegetation. Thistles, seeds, twigs or burrs can become entangled in the wool and are very difficult to remove. You will not want to be spending your precious spinning time picking them out.

Skirtings: Check that the fleece has been well skirted. Skirtings are the edges of the fleece which are dirty and contain more grease. They are not suitable for spinning. They are usually removed at time of shearing leaving the main body of the fleece for the spinner.

Soundness

A sheep which has been in poor health may produce a 'tender' fleece which means the staples will lack strength and have a "break" across its width. You can easily check for breaks by holding a staple firmly with two hands and pulling it taut. You should hear a 'pinging' sound. If there is tenderness the staple is likely to pull apart.

Discolouration

Avoid fleeces that have a stain. The most common stain is a yellow colour called 'canary' which is caused by climatic conditions or vegetation and cannot be washed out. Test the fleece by washing a few staples in cool water.

In summary

Your first fleece needs to be clean, well skirted, have a 10-12cm (4-5ins) staple length with even crimp, be sound and have good colour (no staining). All of these qualities will ensure you have a fleece with a good yield, that is, the weight of usable wool. I would recommend a Romney or Corriedale of 30-34 microns.

Sorting a fleece

Whilst the best wool for hand spinning is found on the shoulder and sides, all parts of the fleece are useful. It's a good idea to sort your fleece soon after purchase and before spinning or storing.

- Use a protective floor covering and lay the fleece out in a well-lit area with the cut end down and the tips facing up.
- Discard any skirtings that are still present.
- Remove any portions that are matted or have a lot of vegetation.
- Make a separate pile of belly, neck and britch wool if present. These areas will have a shorter and coarser staple and can be used for other projects such as felting, stuffing cushions or spun separately for hard-wearing garments.

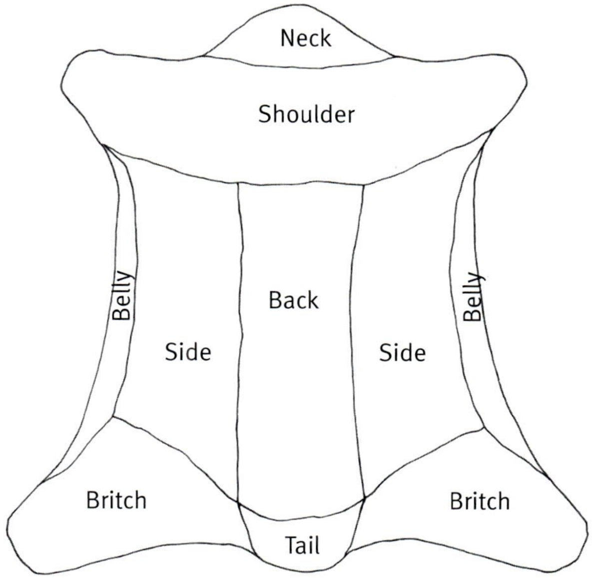

Parts of a fleece

- Check the centre back portion which has been exposed to the weather. These staples may be tender, shorter in staple length or have excessive dirt and vegetation and almost always need removing.
- Discard any second cuts that may be present as these are very short and not suitable for spinning.
- A coloured fleece may provide you with a beautiful range of colours which you may wish to sort into shades for spinning separately.

Fleece storage

Calico bags are great for fleece storage as they allow the wool to breathe and at the same time keep insects out. Cardboard boxes lined with newspaper are also fine. I do not recommend using plastic bags as these cause the fleece to sweat which will create condensation and possible matting of the wool.

Remember to label the bags with the breed, weight, and if you wish, the portion of the fleece. Store your wool in a cool place.

To wash or not to wash in preparation for spinning

Fleece can be spun washed (scoured), or unwashed (in the grease). This is very much a personal choice and every new spinner will benefit from experiencing both methods.

When washing fleece, avoid excessive soap and agitation which will cause the wool to felt. Ensure the fibre is thoroughly dried before it is stored as damp wool may attract mould and bacteria.

Spinning in the grease

Spinners who enjoy spinning in the grease love the feel of a freshly shorn fleece and the lanolin on their hands. The fibres are free-flowing and often require only the minimum of preparation – just a little teasing out with the fingers. There is no washing required.

Clean, greasy spinning

If you find the smell of raw wool unappealing but would like to spin with the natural grease, gently washing your fleece in cool water will remove any offensive smells and dirt but retain the grease giving you clean, greasy wool.

Method: Place 170-200gm (6-8ozs) of staples in a plastic basket or mesh bag with the tips facing in the same direction. This helps with separating them after washing.

Submerge into a tub of cold water and soak for 2-3 hours. Drain the tub and gently press to remove excess water. Repeat the wash once more, then rinse in cool water for about an hour.

Remove the staples, wrap in a towel and remove excess water by either rolling up the towel and either squeezing tightly or using the spin cycle on your washing machine. Lay out flat to dry.

Washing (scouring)

There are times when a fleece will need to be thoroughly washed in hot water to remove the grease. A fleece with excessive dirt or grease will be much more pleasant to spin if it is washed.

Fleece that is to be dyed should be washed as greasy wool does not take up dye well.

The wool should be washed if it is to be hand or drum carded. These tools can become badly soiled if used with greasy fleece and will be very difficult to clean.

Staples ready for washing

Submerging the staples in hot water

Method: Use this method to wash fleeces with no wax content, ie medium and coarse breeds. Place 170-200gm (6-8ozs) of staples (or your skeins) in a plastic basket or mesh bag with the tips facing in the same direction. This helps with separating them after washing.

Submerge the basket or bag into a tub of hot, soapy water using about 55ml (3tbsps) of a mild washing powder, liquid detergent or pure soap flakes that have been dissolved.

Soak for about an hour, drain the tub and gently press to remove excess water. Repeat the wash once more, then rinse in warm water three times or until the water is clean. Remove the staples, wrap in a towel and remove excess water by rolling up the towel and either squeezing tightly or using the spin cycle on your washing machine. Lay out flat to dry.

Oil mixture

Washing a fleece will remove its natural grease. It can be re-oiled if desired prior to spinning by spraying on a mixture of one part olive oil and one part water, or one part neatsfoot oil and one part water. Wrap the wool in a towel and leave for several hours to allow the oil to penetrate but do not leave it on too long as the oil will turn rancid.

Washing fleeces with a high wax content – Merino, Polwarth, Corriedale

These fleeces need to be washed in very hot water with plenty of soap to thoroughly remove the very high wax and grease content they contain. To prevent the residual wax and grease setting in the fibre, avoid letting the water cool down during the washing and rinsing process.

Sort the fleece into staples of finger-thickness and place about 100gm (4ozs) in a plastic basket or mesh bag with the tips facing in the same direction. The staples will lose up to half their weight in the washing process. Washing smaller amounts at a time will allow the water to penetrate deep into the staples for thorough removal of the wax and grease.

Half fill a tub with the hottest water from the tap and add about 55ml (3tbsps) of a mild washing powder, liquid detergent or pure soap flakes. Make sure the soap flakes have dissolved completely before adding the wool. Submerge the basket or bag into the water and press down gently. Soak for about 30 minutes, remove from the tub. Assess how clean the fibre is and if necessary, repeat the wash.

All wax and grease must be totally removed before spinning otherwise the yarn may feel sticky and not soft.

Rinse in warm water, not cold, two or three times until the water is clear. Roll the staples in a towel to remove excess water and then leave to dry and work their magic. The staples will puff up considerably as they dry and beckon to be spun!

Weather damage is confined to the tip and these can easily be removed by either cutting, pulling off after washing, or flick carding. Removing the tip reduces pilling which is caused by short fibres working their way to the surface and rubbing into small, semi-felted clumps of fibre.

Spinning with wool

The fibre diameter of wool is measured in microns (a micron is a millionth of a metre). The lower the micron number, the finer the wool. Each fleece has a natural thickness and elasticity of spun yarn. If you are not sure how thick to spin the wool, let the fleece guide you. The crimp or wave pattern in a wool staple will reveal much about how the fibre should be spun. A fleece with a tight crimp and fine fibres will need a lot of twist and will produce a fine, soft yarn whereas a fleece with very little crimp will only need a small amount of twist and will spin a thick, coarse yarn.

The number of crimps per cm (in) in the staple and twists per cm (in) in the single are related. If they match, then you are spinning to the natural characteristics of that fleece. Take the time to make two or three samples before you begin your project. Your yarn will be easier to spin and feel better if you spin to suit the fleece.

Merino

Merino

18-25 micron, staple length 6.5-10cm ($2^1/_2$-4ins)

Merino is a very soft wool with a closely spaced crimp and firm staples with a blunt tip. The wool has a high wax and grease content and will need thorough washing in hot water to remove completely for ease of drafting.

Preparation: To reduce pilling, remove the tips by cutting them off. Hand card for a woollen yarn. Flick card for a worsted yarn.

Spinning: It is beneficial to have some spinning experience to make the most of the special qualities of Merino wool. Spin a fine woollen yarn using the long draw, or a worsted yarn using a short draw. Spin with a very light bobbin tension. Fine fibres like Merino need plenty of twist.

Uses: Suitable for knitted baby wear, evening stoles, shawls and scarves, woven garments, blankets and felting.

Polwarth

Polwarth

23-26 micron, staple length 7.5-12.5cm (3-5ins) (Cross of 3/4 Merino and 1/4 Lincoln)

Polwarth is lofty, elastic and next-to-skin soft. The Merino ancestry gives the fibre its softness and fineness and the Lincoln, a good staple length. The staples are silkier and creamier than Merino and have a well defined crimp. It is a waxy wool and will need a thorough wash in hot water before spinning.

Preparation: Flick card for a worsted yarn and hand card for a woollen yarn. Polwarth is lovely blended with other fine fibres of a similar length, such as angora, alpaca and silk.

Spinning: The wool is soft and free-flowing making it easier to spin than Merino. Spin a fine worsted or woollen yarn with a light tension and a good amount of twist.

Uses: Suitable for knitted baby wear, evening stoles, shawls and scarves, woven garments and blankets. Good for felting.

Corriedale

Corriedale

26-33 micron, staple length 7.5-12.5cm (3-5ins)

Corriedale is my favourite fleece for spinning. The staples have a clear, even crimp pattern and open up easily during carding and flow smoothly while spinning. There is some wax content in the wool due to this breed being a cross between Merino and either English Leicester or Lincoln. Wash well in hot water before spinning.

Preparation: Flick card for a worsted yarn. Hand card for a woollen yarn. Drum card for a semi-worsted or woollen yarn using a fine drum carder.

Spinning: Fine to medium woollen, worsted or semi-worsted. Corriedale will bulk after washing and has good elasticity.

Uses: Suitable for medium weight knitted, woven and crocheted outer garments, rugs, blankets and cushions.

Dorset Down

Dorset Down

26-29 micron, staple length 5-7.5cm (2-3ins)

Dorset Down is a spongy, crisp wool with no apparent crimp in the staple, but individual fibres are crimped.

Preparation: Hand or drum card for a woollen yarn. Blend with other wools to increase elasticity.

Spinning: The short staples of this breed are perfect for spinning a true woollen yarn that will full well.

Uses: Ideal for springy knitwear giving excellent shape retention. The woollen yarn gives soft, full fabrics that will be crease resistant and light but warm. Great for travel rugs, blankets and socks.

Romney

Romney

31-38 micron, staple length 12.5-17.5cm (5-7ins)

Romney is the general purpose sheep of New Zealand. With open staples of a good length, it is an excellent choice for beginners. For ease of carding and spinning, look for a fleece with a well-defined crimp pattern and a staple length of 10-15cm (5-6ins). The staples are firm with a pointed tip and the wool is lustrous. It has little bulk after washing.

Preparation: Flick card for a worsted yarn. Hand card for a woollen yarn. Drum card for a semi-worsted or woollen yarn.

Spinning: Woollen, worsted or semi-worsted.

Uses: A mature fleece is well-suited to hard-wearing knitted, woven or crocheted outer garments, upholstery fabrics and cushions. Choose a hogget (first year) fleece for finer knitted or woven garments.

Gotland

Gotland

27-33 micron, staple length 15-20cm (6-8ins)

Gotland is a silky, lustrous soft wool in a range of grey shades from silver to black. Called Gotland Pelt in their native Sweden. The staples have a regular S-shaped wavy appearance in well-defined locks. Low bulk.

Preparation: Flick card for a worsted yarn. Hand card for a woollen yarn.

Spinning: Spin fine worsted or woollen yarns. A worsted yarn will enhance the sheen and produce soft-draping, delicate garments.

Uses: Woven and knitted garments - wraps, jackets, scarves and shawls. Excellent for felting.

English Leicester

English Leicester

37-40 micron, staple length 15-20cm (6-8ins)

English Leicester has long and lustrous staples of even length and fibre diameter, with a well-defined crimp. The staples are firm with a pointed tip.

Preparation: Flick card for a worsted yarn. Drum card using a coarse drum carder.

Spinning: Well suited for thicker yarns using a moderate amount of twist and a short draw. Plying enhances the sheen.

Uses: Hard wearing outer garments, floor rugs, upholstery, wall hangings and braids.

Lincoln

Lincoln

38-44 micron, staple length 17.5-25cm (7-10ins)

Lincoln is a strong, lustrous wool. The staples are very firm with a spiral crimp and a large curl at the tip.

Preparation: Flick card for a worsted yarn. Drum card using a carder with coarse teeth. Finer fleeces can be blended successfully with mohair.

Spinning: Worsted or semi-worsted yarn using a short draw.

Uses: Hard wearing outer garments, floor rugs, upholstery and wall hangings.

Coloured sheep

Black and coloured wool

Today high-quality coloured sheep are kept for their wool and there is a wide range of colours from grey through to black, and brown (also called moorit).

Coloured wool adds another dimension to hand spinning. The natural variation in many fleeces provides flexibility for the hand spinner. You may choose to spin the colours randomly for a naturally striped garment or sort the colours for spinning separately. For a subtle colour variation in your project, try blending all the colours in the fleece with hand carders or a drum carder.

Naturally coloured wool is ideal for blending with other fibres such as mohair or alpaca, giving the end product a touch of luxury. A blend of Polwarth, alpaca and silk for example would be a delight to spin for a special garment.

Angora rabbit

Angora

Angora fibre comes from the angora rabbit. The fibres are very fine and soft. They are straight, slippery and lack elasticity. Angora fibre is less dense than other fibres therefore it takes a lot more to equal the weight of the same volume of fibre such as wool or mohair. Only a small proportion is needed in a blend for its softness to be felt. Angora dyes well.

It is usually very clean and requires no washing or carding.

Preparation: Angora can be spun on its own or blended with other fibres, such as wool, alpaca or mohair, using fine hand carders or a drum carder.

Spinning: The short, slippery fibres are a challenge to spin, needing very little tension and plenty of twist. Use the small or medium whorl on your wheel and the short forward draft to make a worsted yarn. Angora garments are known for their fuzziness which is not apparent while spinning. It appears after the yarn has been washed and handled. The ends of the fibres work their way to the surface and create a fuzzy halo effect.

End uses: Garments made from 100% angora are very warm. Hats, scarves, mittens, gloves and baby garments would be ideal. A sweater would be best made from a blend of say 30% angora, 70% wool.

Suri (left and centre) and Huacaya alpacas

Alpaca

Alpaca is a relative of the llama. There are two types – Suri and Huacaya. The Suri has long, straight fibres which are silky, very fine, very soft and lustrous. The Huacaya has shorter fibres and a natural crimp. It is soft and easy to spin. Alpacas produce a lovely variety of natural colours in their fleeces: white, grey, light and dark browns, reddish brown and black.

Alpaca fibre is strong, very warm, lightweight and durable. It has little or no elasticity, drapes well and does not pill. It takes dye well too. Alpaca fibre can be purchased as raw fleece, commercially carded roving or combed top. It does not contain any natural grease and can be carded and spun unwashed or washed. If you prefer washed fibre, a gentle soak in lukewarm water with a mild detergent is enough to remove the dirt. Let the fibre soak for about 20-30 minutes then gently squeeze out the excess water. Rinse in lukewarm water and remove the excess by rolling in a towel. Lay out flat to dry.

Huacaya alpaca

Huacaya preparation: Huacaya is well suited to hand carding into rolags for a soft woollen spin for knitting or weaving. It can also be drum carded, and is ideal for blending with other fibres such as wool, silk, angora and mohair. Blending with wool will give the yarn some elasticity, silk will add more lustre and mohair or angora will give it a fluffy look. Use carding tools with fine teeth for best results.

Huacaya spinning: Alpaca fibre is smooth and lacking in bulk and therefore needs a little more twist in the singles and plying to give it stability. Too much twist can cause the yarn to feel stringy so it's a good idea to make a sample to check the result. Use a medium draft or the long draw for a light, airy woollen yarn.

Suri preparation: Although Suri fibre can be successfully hand carded if the locks are not too long, I prefer to tease open the fibre with my fingers and prepare carded batts using a fine drum carder. Feed the fibre on in small amounts and turn the handle slowly and steadily. Two passes are enough to make a beautiful, easy to spin batt.

Suri spinning: The carded batts are very easy to draft using the short forward draw and a very light tension on the bobbin for a beautiful, lustrous, fine worsted yarn. As the Suri fibres are dense, try and spin very fine singles otherwise the plied yarn may be heavy and the finished garment will sag. Hand spun Suri yarns are very well suited to lace knitting or weaving.

End uses: Alpaca spins into a lovely soft yarn for knitting and makes a good warp for weaving if a little more twist is added. It can also be felted into scarves, hats, vests or wraps.

Suri alpaca

Silk

Silk is pure luxury. As soon as you touch the fine, soft fibres, you know that it is a very special and magical fibre.

Silk is produced from the cocoons of silkworms and is the most lustrous of natural fibres. There are two types of silk for hand spinning. Bombyx Mori is pure white and is produced from silk worms which have fed on mulberry leaves. Tussah silk is a golden tan colour and comes from silkworms which have fed on oak leaves.

Silk has many qualities. As well as its natural sheen, it is strong, resistant to pilling, and the long fibres make it easy to spin. It looks stunning when dyed and blends beautifully with other fibres such as wool, cashmere, mohair and alpaca.

Combed top: Silk is usually prepared as combed top for hand spinning. The fibres are carded and combed into a parallel arrangement. The fibre is easier to handle and spin if it is divided into three or four strips and then pre-drafted for spinning.

Spinning: The golden rule for spinning silk is to handle the fibre very lightly. Any moisture on your hands may cause the fibres to compact a little and drafting will be more difficult. Use the short forward or backward draft for a smooth, shiny worsted yarn. Spin with just enough tension to draw the yarn onto the bobbin.

Silk needs to be firmly spun but not overtwisted as this may cause the yarn to lose its lustre and feel stringy. Select a higher ratio on your wheel if you need to add more twist, or treadle a little faster. Ply firmly.

Although silk fibres are very fine, this does not mean you must spin a very fine yarn. Spin it to the thickness and style you need for your project.

Tussah is easier to spin than Bombyx Mori as the staple length is similar to wool and the fibres have a slight texture to the surface. The long, slippery Bombyx Mori fibres require more control and a very light tension on the bobbin.

Wash the skeins in warm water with a gentle detergent and delicate hand movements. Rinse carefully and then remove excess water by gently squeezing, never wringing, then rolling in a towel to remove excess moisture. Adding a little vinegar to the rinse helps to enhance the sheen.

Silk caps and hankies: Silk caps and hankies are made from cultivated cocoons that are not suitable for reeling because of discolouration or damage. Several cocoons are degummed and stretched over a frame so that each cap or hankie has several layers. Caps are stretched over a bell-shaped frame and hankies over a square frame.

The fibres are very fine and will catch on any rough spots on your hands. It is a good idea to apply hand cream before you begin working with them. You may need to re-apply at regular intervals while preparing the fibre.

Spinning from multi-layered silk preparations would be almost impossible because the fibres are almost a continuous thread and are very strong. It is necessary to separate the layers and then stretch into a thin roving for spinning.

Left: Bombyx Mori silk
Centre: Tussah silk
Right: Dyed Tussah silk – navajo plied

Silk caps

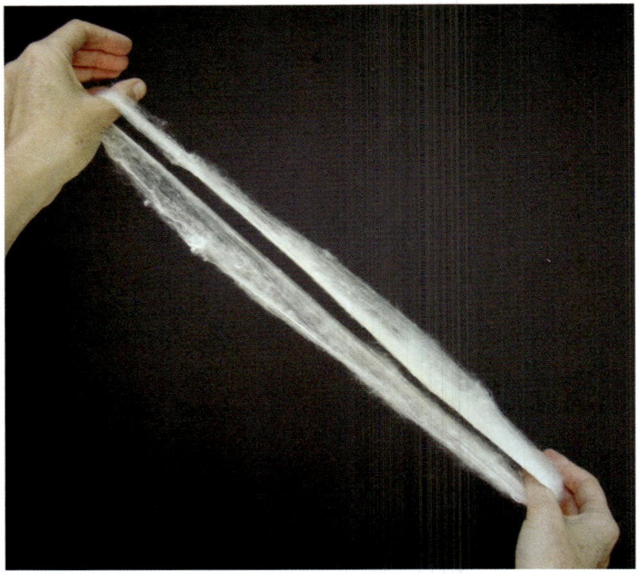

Stretching out the cap

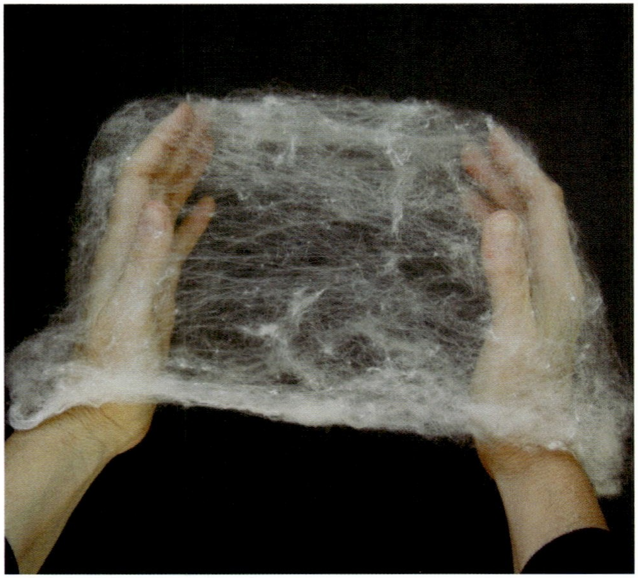

One cap ready for stretching into a roving

Caps: Lay the cap flat on a table with the dome at the top, smoothing it out if it has been folded or wrinkled. You will see that the edge is not one piece, but is made up of many layers that are thicker than the rest of the silk.

Find a thin spot along this dense ridge and pick at the edge with your fingernail until you can separate one layer. Slowly peel it back all the way around from the edge toward the dome then twist off the tiny filaments still attached.

To stretch this layer into a roving, make a hole in the centre of the layer. Place your thumbs through the hole and pull your two hands apart slowly and steadily to make a large circle of fibre. When your arms won't stretch any further, use your hands to stretch it to your desired thickness.

Keep your hands about 30cm (12ins) or more apart. I like to stretch the fibre out to a roving approximately 2.5cm (1in) wide. When you are satisfied with the length of your roving, break the circle and wind it into a very loose ball ready for spinning.

Because of the very long fibres, this type of silk is harder on your hands to draft for spinning than combed top. The finer the roving, the easier it is to draft.

Hankies: Preparing silk hankies for spinning is much the same as silk caps. Look at the dense ridge around the edges and find the least compacted corner. Pick at the edge until you can peel away one layer. Once you have a thin layer, stretch it into a rectangle and keep stretching it out lengthwise until it is as thin as you would like.

Spinning the rovings: Set your wheel for the lightest possible tension. Tie the end of the roving to the leader with a knot to prevent it slipping off. The fibre from caps and hankies will not draft as easily as combed top. Because the tension on your wheel is very light, you will need your front hand to pinch hard on the fibre to provide the tension to draft against. As the fibres are very long, your drafting hand will be well back behind your forward hand by about 30cm (12ins).

Sometimes the drafting will feel effortless and sometimes you will need to use some strength. Slubs and short fibres can be removed by picking them out if necessary.

The dense edges of silk caps and hankies will be distributed along the length of your roving giving you a textured, interesting yarn. Try dyeing caps and hankies with three or four colours. When you stretch them out, there will interesting colour changes along the length of the yarn.

End uses: Silk singles make an excellent warp in weaving due to their strength. Woven scarves and shawls look stunning and have wonderful drape.

Plied yarns make beautiful knitted or crocheted garments, however, keep in mind that silk has no elasticity and garments will be soft and drape well. Use your hand spun silk for embroidery too.

Dyed silk hankies

Hank spun from the dyed hankies

Mohair

Mohair fibre comes from Angora goats and is white, silky and lustrous. The long fibres make it easy to spin. Kid mohair is the first shearing from a young angora goat and is very fine and soft. Goatling is the second shearing and is also fine and soft. Adult mohair is from the mature goat and can range from fine to coarse. Mohair has less elasticity than wool, is strong, wrinkle resistant and takes dye beautifully.

It is readily available in sliver form for easy spinning but if you wish to use a fresh fleece, choose a well-skirted one that doesn't have lots of tangles. Separate the fleece into individual locks and soak in hot water with a mild liquid detergent for about an hour to remove the grease. Remove the excess water by wrapping in a towel and either squeezing it out with your hands or use the spin cycle on your washing machine.

Preparation: A light card with a flick carder is enough to prepare the staples for spinning. Mohair is ideal for blending with wool using hand carders or the drum carder. Use at least 30-40% mohair to retain its lustre.

Spinning: It is best spun into a soft, fluffy yarn using a light tension and a woollen spin using the long draw or a semi-worsted spin using the medium draw. If spun with too much twist the yarn will feel like string. You need just enough twist to hold it together.

Weaving with mohair: When you weave with mohair as a warp, sett it further apart than you would with wool of a similar thickness. A close sett may cause the warp threads to tangle with each other making it difficult to obtain a good shed. To help open the shed for the next beat, change the shed after you beat but before you move the beater back.

End Uses: Mohair can be knitted into coats, dresses, sweaters, hats, scarves, shawls, mittens and socks. In weaving, it is perfect for throws, blankets, wraps and fabric lengths for apparel.

Top: Dyed mohair skein
Bottom: Angora goat

Tencel

Tencel is the trademarked brand name for the fibre lyocell.

Lyocell is made from wood pulp cellulose by dissolving the wood pulp with a non-toxic solvent. The dissolved pulp is forced through tiny holes called spinnerets which create long, smooth, lustrous fibres much like silk in appearance.

Lyocell is a versatile fibre with many desirable properties. Lustre, soft drape, absorbency and comfortable to wear against the skin. It blends well with other fibres such as wool, alpaca, silk and cotton and can be dyed to a deep colour using fibre-reactive dyes.

It is very strong when wet making it suitable for hand or machine washing and tumble drying. When wet it can become stiff and board-like, however, this improves as the yarn or fabric dries. Softness and drape can be enhanced by tumble drying on low heat with a towel for a few minutes.

Spinning: As it is a manufactured fibre, the staple length can vary. The fibre sourced for the sample in the photograph has a staple length of 10cm (4ins), allowing easy spinning. The fibres flow smoothly if the sliver is divided and pre-drafted.

To retain its luscious sheen, use a short forward draft and plenty of twist. If less twist is used, the yarn may become fluffy with wear as lyocell can fibrillate which means the fibre ends can splinter to form tiny "hairs" on the surface.

End Uses: Hand spun Tencel looks stunning in handwoven scarves or shawls with its superb drape and sheen. For shape retention in knitted garments, try blending with fine wool such as Merino or Corriedale.

Bamboo

Bamboo fibre from the bamboo plant has many special qualities. This natural cellulose fibre is biodegradable and has anti-bacterial properties making it especially suitable for people with skin allergies.

The fibres have micro-gaps and holes which allow it to breathe, making it extremely cool to wear, never sticking to the skin in hot weather. Knitted or woven textiles are very soft, smooth and have lovely drape.

Preparation: Raw bamboo fibre can be blended with cotton, silk or Tencel using hand carders.

Spinning: Spinning the raw fibre is much like spinning cotton, giving texture to the finished yarn. Use the long draw and plenty of twist.

Commercially prepared sliver is very easy to spin by pre-drafting the sliver. Spin with plenty of twist using the short forward draft to produce a smooth, shiny worsted yarn.

End uses: Suitable for knitting outer garments as well as garments to be worn next to the skin. In weaving, bamboo fabric has excellent drape for scarves and shawls, and because of its natural anti-bacterial property, is especially good for hand towels.

Cotton

Cotton comes from the cotton plant and the first thing you notice about it is that the fibres are very short, ranging from 2-5cm ($^3/_4$-2ins).

Commercially carded cotton sliver is available, however you can prepare raw fibre by making a puni which is similar to a woollen rolag. You will need hand carders with fine teeth and a puni stick which is made from a 6mm ($^1/_4$in) dowel.

Preparation: Hand card the cotton using a very light stroke, being careful to keep the cotton on top of the carders and not pressed into the teeth. When carding is complete, remove the fibre by placing the puni stick at the toe of carder and roll the fibre firmly around the stick towards the heel. Remove the stick. Make several punis in preparation for spinning.

Spinning: Because the fibres are so short, they will need a lot of twist to hold them together. Loosen the bobbin tension and use the smallest whorl to give the maximum amount of twist.

Spin using the long draw. If you haven't used this method of drafting, practise with wool first to get a feel for it. Remember to let plenty of twist accumulate when you are spinning cotton. If the fibre breaks regularly, let the twist build up before feeding the yarn onto the bobbin. Adjust the tension if necessary to ensure there is enough for you to draft against as well as enabling the yarn to wind on.

Spinning raw cotton will produce a more textured yarn than spinning from a roving.

For an unusual yarn, try blending cotton with a longer fibre such as silk or wool (or both) on the drum carder. Use the technique described on page 46 to sandwich the cotton between two layers of another fibre. You will need to card the batt several times for a thorough blend but the result will be delightful to spin. Draw the batt out lengthwise to create a thin roving for spinning. Add plenty of twist to ensure the short cotton fibres are secured.

End uses: Hand spun cotton is ideal for crochet and knitted garments and makes a great yarn for weaving tableware.

Flax

Flax fibre comes from the flax plant Linum usitatissimum, an erect annual plant growing to 1.2m (4ft) tall, with slender stems. It has been grown for thousands of years for both its seeds and fibres. Various parts of the plant have been used to make fabric, dye, paper, medicines, fishing nets and soap. It is also grown as an ornamental plant in gardens, producing pale blue flowers.

The flax fibre is located in the stalk, beneath the outer surface between the outer bark and the woody, pithy inner core of the stem. The fibres run from the root of the plant to the tip and vary in length from about 5 to 40cm (2-16ins). Flax which has been spun is called linen.

Flax plants have short roots and are harvested by pulling out of the ground rather than cutting. The stalks are stored in bundles for drying. They are then put through a process called rippling which removes the seeds. The stalks are then wet-retted, a process which rots the outer core of the stalks to expose the fibres.

The final process before spinning is hackling – a combing process where the short fibres, called tow, are removed from the long fibres, called stricks. Stricks and tow are the most common forms of flax for hand spinning.

The traditional method of spinning flax stricks is from a distaff, a long vertical pole that can be attached to your spinning wheel. A bundle of long flax fibres are attached to the distaff from which the spinner drafts. Flax can also be spun from prepared sliver which is held on your lap as you would for normal spinning.

Flax single

Preparation of flax for distaff spinning: Break off a length of flax approximately 45cm (18ins) long. Tie the fibres together at one end. Fan the fibres out, working back and forth across the bundle letting the fibres cross over each other. After fanning, untie the fibre and wind the fan onto the distaff. Beginning at the top of the distaff, secure the flax with ribbon or cord, crossing over as you work to the bottom.

Spinning: Spin with a light tension and just a little twist. For a smooth, strong yarn, moisten your fingers as you spin. Keep a small container of water beside the spinning wheel and moisten your fingers regularly. Spinning the fibre with dry fingers will produce a hairy, textured yarn.

End uses: Flax is a harsh, hard-wearing, non-elastic fibre, which softens with use and age. It has a crisp handle which makes it more suitable for weaving than knitting or crochet. Singles are ideal for hand woven tableware.

For a softer and more elastic yarn, try plying one single of flax with a single of wool.

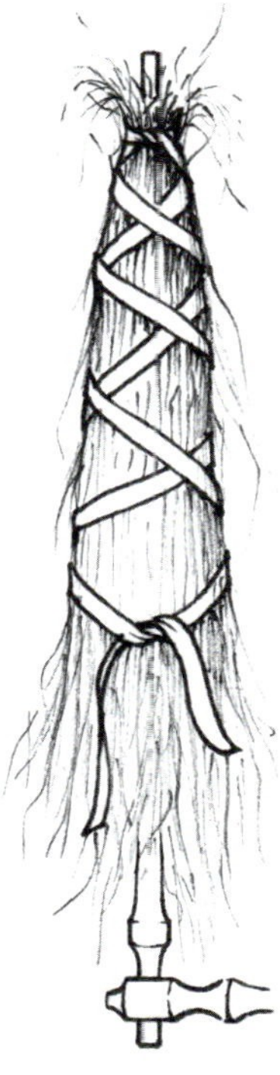

Flax wound onto the distaff ready for spinning

Distaff attached to the Ashford Traditional wheel

Soybean

If you enjoy spinning smooth worsted yarns, you will find soybean fibre enjoyable to spin. This fibre is made from the residue of soybeans from tofu manufacturing. It has moisture absorption and ventilation properties along with beautiful drape, softness and warmth.

Preparation and spinning: Soybean sliver is available in roving form with a staple length between 7-10cm (2^3/$_4$-4ins). Split the roving to a pencil thickness for spinning. Keep your hands approximately 10cm (4ins) apart.

Spinning: Spinning the sliver is similar to spinning silk top. Use the short forward or back draft for a strong, worsted yarn.

Finishing: To set the twist for a plied yarn, soak in warm water then gently squeeze out the excess water by rolling in a towel. Place your hands inside the skein and 'snap' to realign the yarn.

End uses: A plied, balanced yarn would be lovely in any knitting or weaving project.

Commercially prepared fibre

Commercially carded fibre is a wonderful convenience for today's spinners and comes in three forms – sliver, roving and combed top. There is no sorting or washing, no waste and you can start spinning right away. However, as with fleece wool, there are certain qualities you will want to look for:

- Breed – Because the wool has been carded, most of the fibres will have been arranged parallel to each other which means the crimp and length of staple will not be obvious. There is usually a label on the bag with the name of the breed and often the micron number. Do ask the supplier if this information is not available. You can check the staple length by gently pulling on the end of the sliver until it separates from the rest. The length that comes off will be the original staple length of the fleece which is not altered during the carding process.
- The sliver should have the fibres evenly distributed throughout. Hold it up to the light and check for any clumpy areas.
- Check that there is no vegetation in the sliver and as with fleece, try and see all the fibre, if possible, right down to the bottom of the bag.

Sliver: Carded fibre which has been drawn into a long, thin strip to align the fibres for either semi-worsted or woollen spinning.

Roving: The same as sliver, except slightly thicker and the fibre is drawn out further and given a slight twist for semi-worsted or woollen spinning.

Combed top: The fibres are combed in one direction, from butt end to tip, to keep the fibres parallel for true worsted spinning. Usually combed using long fibre wool.

These prepared forms of fibre can become compacted in their packaging. Spinning will be easier if they are pre-drafted a little before spinning.

Novelty yarns

Novelty yarns are yarns with character. They are a lot of fun to spin and the perfect way to let your creative side go wild as you experiment with texture, colour and different fibres. Novelty yarns are usually constructed of two or three singles using either handspun yarn or a combination of handspun and millspun yarns and can be produced from worsted or woollen yarns. This is great way to learn more about twist direction, drive ratio and further develop coordination and hand movement at the wheel.

Because most novelty yarns take longer to ply than a standard two-ply yarn, they are plied using the large whorl on your wheel to produce a balanced yarn. For consistent results and better control with special techniques, use a lazy kate placed well behind you during plying to allow the yarn to travel freely and directly into the orifice.

Freshly plied novelty yarns are often very 'energised' and benefit from resting on the bobbin for about 24 hours before skeining and washing to set the twist.

Sampling is an essential part of creating novelty yarns and is time well spent. A lot more work will go into them and you will want to be sure it is what you really want. Knit, crochet or weave the sample and keep a note of what you did throughout the entire process. At a later date you might wish to use one of your samples as a basis for a new novelty yarn.

I used the Ashford Traditional spinning wheel to spin the skeins shown in the following pages.

Knot yarn

A knot yarn, sometimes called seed yarn, is a two-ply yarn where small bumps are made by letting one single wrap back and forth on itself while the other single is held under a small amount of tension.

One single is held back while a knot is made with the other. Extra twist is required in both singles because while the knot is being made, twist is being removed from the tensioned yarn.

Make the knots alternately from each yarn.

There are many exciting possibilities for creating knot yarns for knitting or weaving. Here are few suggestions and considerations:

- Spin one single of a solid colour and the other a multi-coloured sliver. There will be many different coloured knots along the yarn.
- Spin one single of wool and the other of another fibre, such as silk, angora or alpaca. Silk will give lovely shiny knots and angora, softer looking knots.
- Use one millspun single and one handspun single to save time.
- Ply two knot yarns together for a very textured yarn in knitting.
- In weaving, a knot yarn would look particularly good as a feature in the weft.
- Experiment with the size and spacing of the knots.

Method:

1. Spin two fine singles Z twist using a small whorl.

2. Attach both singles to the leader. Using the large whorl and treadling very slowly, begin plying S twist.

3. To make a knot: Hold one single under a little tension in your back hand. Holding the other single loosely with your front hand, move your hand back and forth, letting the yarn wrap on itself.

4. Continue plying normally until you are ready to make the next knot with the other single.

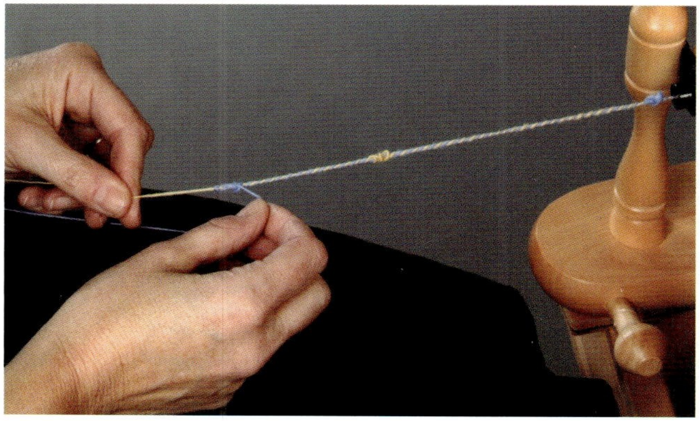

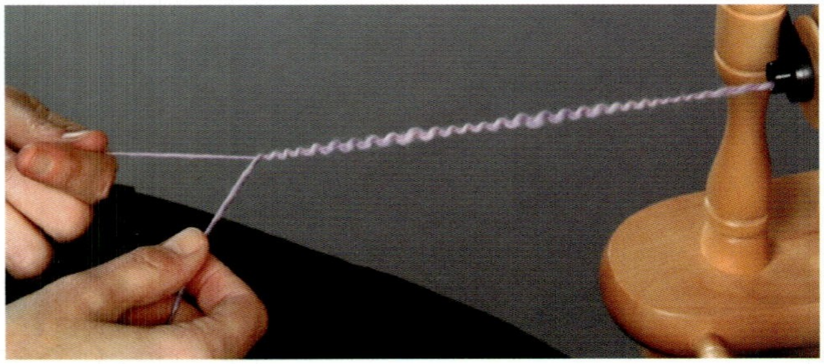

The thick single wrapping around the fine single

Spiral yarn

A spiral yarn comprises two singles, one spun fine – the core yarn, and the other spun thicker – the wrapping yarn. The thick single is allowed to wrap around the fine yarn which is held taut during plying, thus creating a spiral or corkscrew effect.

The core yarn can be a handspun or millspun single. Wool works really well because its hairiness gives the wrapping yarn something to cling onto whereas it will slide around on a smooth, slippery core.

Because the core yarn is held back while the wrapping yarn spirals on, the twist is being removed and it can drift apart. Make sure you have plenty of twist in it to prevent this happening.

The wrapping yarn needs to be at least twice as thick as the core yarn otherwise the finished yarn may just look like uneven plying.

Spiral yarns make lovely weft accents in weaving and will add very subtle texture to the purl side of knitting. They look great when the wrapping yarn is multi-coloured. Make a rolag on hand carders or a batt on the drum carder.

Method:

1. For the core yarn, spin a fine single Z twist using your smallest whorl to give the yarn plenty of twist.

2. For the wrapping yarn, spin a plump single Z twist using medium or large whorl. I used lightly blended hand carded rolags for a light, airy yarn using the largest whorl and a medium draw.

Ply together S twist using your largest whorl as follows:

3. Place the bobbins onto a lazy kate and attach both singles to the leader of an empty bobbin.

4. Hold the core yarn in your back hand under a little tension.

5. Hold the wrapping yarn loosely in your front hand.

6. Treadle slowly and steadily S twist.

7. Let the thick yarn wrap around the core loosely. Allow the core yarn to feed onto the bobbin at regular intervals.

Experiment with the angle at which you let the wrapping yarn wind around the core. The deeper the angle, the more textured the yarn will be.

Bouclé yarn

A bouclé yarn is one which has loops and curls resulting in a very textured yarn. It is a fairly time consuming yarn to spin because the finished yarn is approximately one third the length of the spun yarn. But don't let that put you off. Making a bouclé yarn is extremely rewarding and a fun yarn to make.

Bouclé yarn is a three-ply yarn comprising a core, a wrapper and a binder. The core and wrapper are basically a spiral yarn except the wrapping yarn is pushed towards the orifice from time to time. The completed spiral is then plied with a fine binder which secures the loops and curls that form as the wrapper is slightly loosened.

The core and binder can be handspun or you could use a fine commercial thread. As the wrapping yarn is the focal point of bouclé, I have found sewing thread or a fine millspun yarn to be very suitable for the binder. The wrapping yarn can be just about anything you like. Wool, alpaca, mohair and silk, or a combination of any of these fibres, all work well. A woollen or worsted yarn can be used for the wrapper although a woollen spun yarn produces slightly better loops.

Bouclé yarns make wonderful knitting yarns and are effective in the weft when weaving.

Method:

1. Core yarn – spin a fine single Z twist using a small whorl.

2. Wrapping yarn – spin a fine to medium single Z twist using a medium whorl.

3. Binder yarn (if using handspun) - spin a very fine single S twist using a small to medium whorl.

4. Using the large whorl, make a spiral yarn with the core and wrapping yarn as on the previous page, except this time you will be pushing the wrapping yarn towards the orifice from time to time to cover the core.

5. Attach the spiral and binder yarns to the leader of an empty bobbin and ply Z twist using the large whorl, letting the spiral wrap around the binder loosely.

Variations: Two wrapping yarns of different colours can be spiralled onto the core. This method makes a very lofty bouclé yarn which could be used in small areas of knitting or weaving.

Try using two wrapping yarns of different fibres, for example silk and wool. They will have different amounts of fulling and shrinking when the yarn is washed which will create an interesting effect in the yarn.

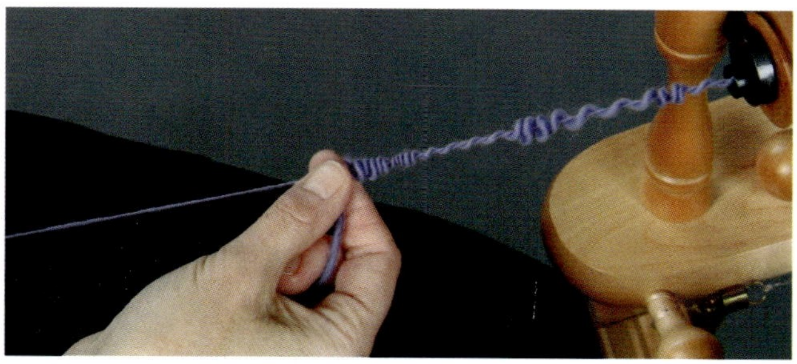

Making a pushed-up spiral yarn

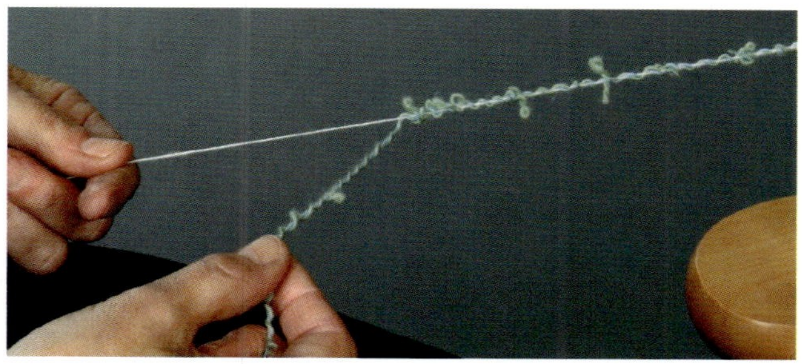

Wrapping the pushed up spiral yarn onto the binder yarn

Slub yarn

Slubs are thick, less twisted areas of fibre placed at random along the length of a fine single. Handspun slub yarns are wonderfully textured and can be used as a single or plied yarn.

If two slub yarns are plied together, the slubs may land on top of each and be too thick to pass through the orifice. This can be overcome by plying with a fine handspun or commercial thread without slubs. Try using a different colour for an interesting effect in the yarn.

Slub singles make great wrapping yarns for a spiral or boucle yarn. Singles are also suitable as a weft in weaving but may be troublesome in the warp as the slubs may catch in the heddles or reed.

To avoid slanting stitches in knitting when using an unbalanced single, the yarn will need to dry under tension to prevent it twisting. Lift the saturated skeins from the bucket or tub and drip-dry, weighting them by hanging a plastic bottle containing a little water.

Try different types of fibre preparation for a variety of effects in the slubs. Woollen spun multi-coloured rolags from hand carders or batts from the drum carder will produce light airy slubs which are more likely to pill, whereas worsted or semi-worsted spun yarn will make a more solid, durable slub.

Method: Use a light tension and treadle slowly for your first effort until you get a feel for making the slubs. Use the large whorl if you feel the twist is getting ahead of your hand movements.

Begin spinning as usual. At the point where you want to insert a slub, pinch the fibre in the drafting zone with your front hand. Continue drafting with your back hand behind the slub. Let go the slub with your front hand. The twist will jump over the slub into the new drafting zone. Continue normal spinning until you want to insert another slub.

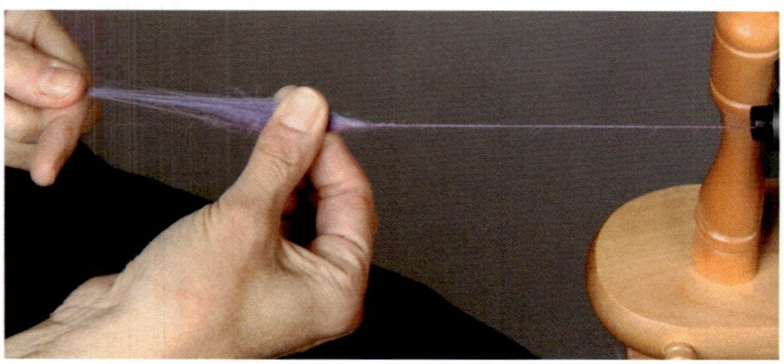

Pinching the fibre in the drafting zone while drafting back behind the slub

Core spinning

This yarn is constructed by letting unspun fibre wrap around a handspun or millspun core yarn. The core yarn can be of any thickness and can be partially or totally covered by the unspun fibre. Core spinning is a great way to use up a yarn that you don't particularly like. If you cover it completely, no-one need ever know what lies beneath! It is also a more efficient way of making a thick, strong yarn than spinning bulky singles as part of the bulk is already provided by the core yarn.

The wrapping fibre can be just about anything you like from natural coloured wool or alpaca to multi-coloured drum carded batts. Experiment with different combinations of core yarns and wrapping fibres and give some thought to the end use of your yarn. For example, a very fine core of wool with a luxurious wrapping of a silk/wool blend would make a delicate yarn suitable for knitting whereas a thick, strong core which has been heavily wrapped could be used for weaving a rug. Core spun yarns can also be crocheted or used to make coiled containers or baskets.

Core spinning is easier if the fibre is open and airy. If using commercial sliver, pre-draft a little. Hand carded rolags or drum carded batts are a joy to use when core spinning.

Method:

1. Use the large whorl and reduce the brake tension on the wheel so that the leader is just pulling on.

2. Attach the core yarn to the leader and hold loosely. It needs to be able to flow freely through your hand.

3. Hold the fibre loosely in your other hand.

4. Begin treadling, allowing the fibre to attach to the core yarn. Keep the core yarn taut to provide tension to draft against. Draft the fibre out at right angles to the core yarn, then let it warp around and feed onto the bobbin.

5. As this yarn is not plied, it is best left on the bobbin for 24 hours before skeining and washing. The hank may need a weight on the end of it during drying to help set the twist.

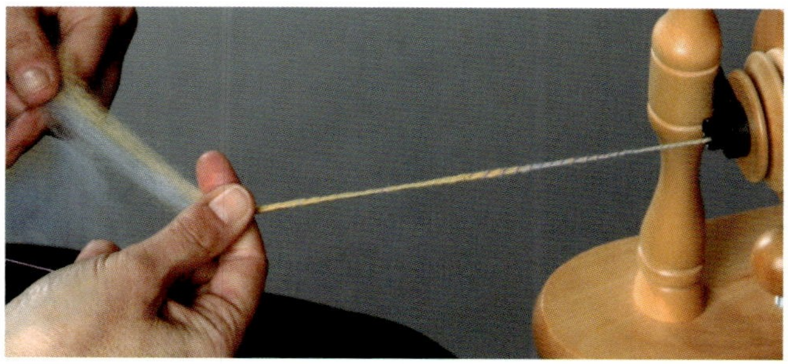

The unspun fibre wrapping around the core yarn

Knitting

One of the most charming aspects of handspun yarn is its originality. Your first yarns are often used for a small knitted item such as a scarf, hat or mittens for which the thickness of yarn is not too important. However, when you are ready to start on a larger project, a little more planning is required.

Most of the time, your hand spun will not match perfectly to the thickness of a suggested commercial yarn in a pattern. To obtain the correct size for your garment, there are two approaches you can take. Firstly, you can try and spin the yarn to match the suggested yarn, or you can alter a pattern to suit the yarn you have spun.

Whichever approach you take, there are some simple measurements you can use to ensure a better fit.

TO MATCH A SUGGESTED YARN IN A PATTERN

Total number of metres or yards: Using this measurement as a guide has proved more accurate for me than trying to match the total weight of yarn required. Handspun yarns can vary considerably in yardage per pound and it is most frustrating to fall short.

Measure each skein by winding a string once around a niddy noddy or whatever device you have chosen to make your skeins. Measure the length of string. After you have wound each skein, count the number of times it has been wound around the niddy noddy and multiply this number by the length of the string.

Attach a label to the skein noting the weight and number of metres or yards. If you have a limited supply of that particular fibre, you will now have a much better idea of how far it will go and be able to plan a project accordingly.

Wraps Per Inch (wpi): This measurement is used to give an approximate weight of yarn (yards per pound) by category, such as lace or bulky. Many millspun yarns are measured this way and have this information on this label Wpi is measured by wrapping your yarn around a ruler for one inch, or by using a specially made wpi gauge which is usually made of wood and has a one inch groove for wrapping the yarn. The yarn is wrapped so that each strand sits snugly beside the next one. They should not overlap, nor should there be any gaps between them. Then count the number of strands to obtain your wpi.

When comparing your handspun yarn to a millspun yarn, use the following chart as a guide. The yards per pound and stitches per inch are approximations and needle sizes are recommended only.

The Ashford Yarn Gauge

Category	Wraps Per Inch (2.5cm)	Yards Per Pound (approx)	Knitting Gauge in stocking stitch per 4ins (10cm)	Recommended Needle Size		
				Metric (mm)	US	UK
Lace	18+	2400+	33-40	2.0 - 2.25	0 - 1	13 - 14
Fingering	16	1800 - 2400	27-32	2.25 - 3.25	1 - 3	10 - 13
Sport	14	1200 - 1800	23-26	3.25 - 3.75	3 - 5	9 - 10
Worsted	12	900 - 1200	16-22	3.75 - 5.5	5 - 9	5 - 9
Bulky	10	600 - 900	12-15	5.5 - 8.0	9 - 11	0 - 5
Very Bulky	8	400 - 600	6-11	8.0+	11+	000 - 0

ALTERING A PATTERN TO SUIT YOUR YARN

Knitting patterns will give you a gauge for the number of stitches and rows per cm (in). I don't worry too much about the row gauge as I just knit to the length required. The important measurement when altering a pattern, is the number of stitches per inch.

The only way to find this is to make a sample by knitting a swatch. This is an essential part of knitting with handspun yarn and will be time well spent as you may need to try two or three needle sizes to achieve the best result. I knit my samples 20 stitches by 20 rows and give it a light wash before taking any measurements as the results may be quite different from that of an unwashed sample.

Let's look at the project on Page 95 as an example. The original pattern for this delightful child's jacket recommends a plied yarn at 13wpi with a gauge of 20sts/10cm(4ins) on size 5mm needles over stocking stitch. This would give a back width measurement of 31.5cm (12½ins).

My yarn is a little thicker at 11wpi and a gauge of 16sts/10cm (4ins). At this gauge the back would measure 37.5cm (14¾ins) which is approximately 20% more than the recommended gauge. The garment would be too big.

I recalculated the number of stitches required by reducing the pattern by 20% as follows:

	Original Pattern	Revised No. of Sts
Back	63	50
Back Neck	23	18
Sleeve	40	32
Each Front	35	28

You may also wish to take measurements from a garment that fits you well and is similar to your intended project. Compare them to those in your pattern and adjust the pattern as required. Once you know the gauge of your handspun yarn, you can do some simple calculations to work out the number of stitches required for each piece of the knitting to obtain a perfect fit every time.

Weaving

A special touch is added to a weaving project that uses your handspun yarn.

When spinning a warp yarn, extra twist is needed to cope with the yarn under tension on the loom as well as friction from the reed and heddles. Plied, worsted yarns are suitable for warps, although singles spun from cotton, or silk hankies or caps, would also be strong enough.

Test the strength of your yarn by trying to break it with your hands. If it drifts apart easily, there is not enough twist. If it is quite difficult to break, then it will be strong enough for a warp. Be careful not to put in so much twist that the yarn becomes hard.

As with knitting, you will need to determine the gauge of your yarn by taking a wraps per inch measurement to work out your sett. A lot of work will go into a handspun, handwoven project so always make a washed and fulled sample before beginning a large project.

Choose fibre that is appropriate for the article to be woven. A finely spun yarn from a strong fleece will never make a soft scarf or shawl. Strong fleece wool would be perfect for rugs, wall hangings and outerwear.

Fine wool, alpaca, silk, angora and bamboo would be good choices for spinning fine yarns to weave scarves and shawls with good drape.

Use textured yarns such as a bouclé or knot yarn for a feature in either warp or weft in scarves, shawls or jackets.

Handspun cotton singles and plied yarns make a good warp or weft in table mats and runners.

For a first project, start with a small item such as a scarf and combine your handspun yarn with a commercial yarn, using one in the warp and the other in the weft.

The classic New Zealand jersey.
A natural coloured handspun jersey in fleece or sliver

Top right: Winter warmer beret. A hand carded blend of autumn colours. Fun to card and easy to spin

Far right: Merino and silk scarf. A luxurious blend using the drum carder and a smooth worsted spun yarn

Bottom right: Child's jacket. A fun to spin project using a different colour blend in each single

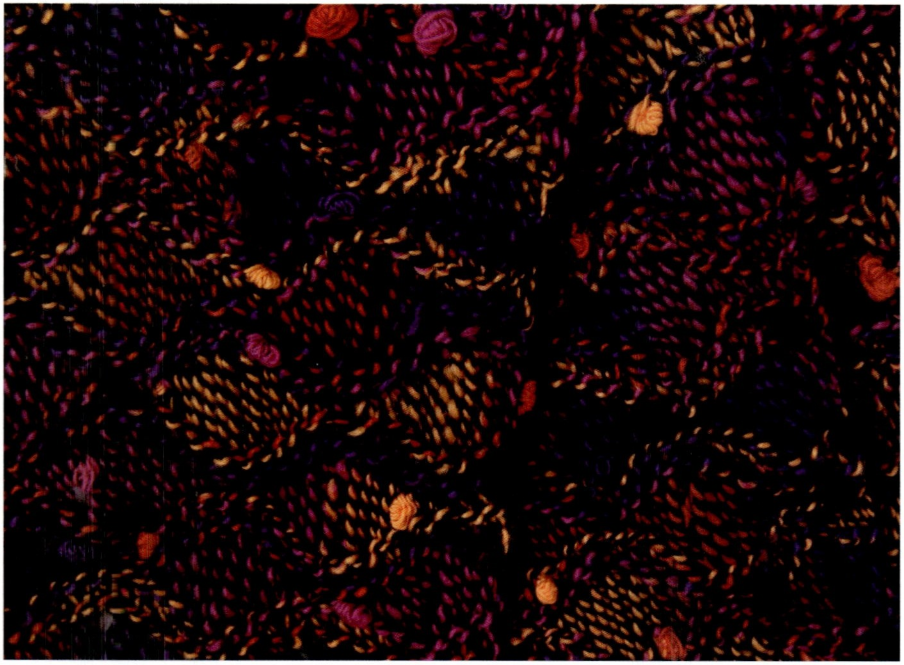

Novelty yarn scarf.
The ridges and medallions in this scarf show off this knot yarn beautifully

Knitting or weaving with your first handspun yarn is an exciting and rewarding experience. It seems like only yesterday that I completed my first skeins and I clearly remember the great sense of satisfaction from my achievements. From raw fleece I had washed, carded and spun enough yarn to make a garment.

Whether you have used fleece or sliver, you will have reached that point too and will be looking for a suitable project for your yarn. The projects on the following pages have been chosen for their simplicity which makes them ideal for practising the carding and spinning techniques you have learned from this book. They will also display the characteristics and uniqueness of your handspun yarn beautifully.

Whether you choose to spin smooth, fine yarns, or highly textured funky yarns, you have now learned the basic skills and can go on to be as creative as you wish. As you gain confidence and experience with your spinning, you will be able to design your own garments, tailoring them to suit your yarn - the only one of its kind.

The classic New Zealand jersey

This classic natural coloured jersey can be spun from unwashed or washed fleece, or one of the natural coloured Ashford slivers. For fleece, choose a soft Romney or Perendale.

You will need:

Needles: 4.5mm (UK7, USA6), 5.5mm (UK5, USA8)

Fleece: You will need approximately 1kg (2.2lbs) of greasy fleece. For a natural look, do not worry about sorting the colours, just take the fleece from the bag as it comes. For a soft, airy yarn, use the medium draw. Ply your singles, taking care not to overply. Wash the hanks following the method on page 52. If you have chosen to wash the fleece, flick card the staples before spinning.

Sliver: 900gm (2lbs) Corriedale sliver

Size: One size fits all. Adjust sleeve and body lengths as required.

Wraps per inch: Approximately 10 wpi when plied into a 2 ply yarn.

Tension: 7 sts to 5cm (2ins) in stocking stitch on 5.5mm needles.

KNITTING THE JERSEY

Back:
Using number 4.5mm needles, cast on 85 sts and k1, p1 rib for 12 rows, increasing 7 sts evenly across the last row (92 sts). Change to 5.5mm needles and work in stocking stitch until back measures 74cm (29ins) or length required.

Shape shoulder:
Cast off 32 sts at the beg of the next 2 rows. Slip remaining 28 sts onto stitch holder.

Front:
Work as for back until front measures 66cm (26ins).
Shape neck:
Next Row: Knit 38, turn.
Next Row: Knit 2 together, knit to end.
Now decrease 1 st at the neck edge on the next 5 rows.
Continue without shaping until front measures same as back to shoulder.

Slip the centre 16 sts onto stitch holder. Join yarn to neck edge and shape as for the first side.

Sleeves:
Using 4.5mm (UK7, USA6) needles cast on 41 sts. Work k1, p1 rib for 12 rows, increasing 4 sts evenly across the last row (45 sts). Change to 5.5mm (UK 5, USA 9) needles.

Continue in stocking stitch increasing 1 st at each end of the 3rd and following 6th rows until there are 71 sts. Work straight until sleeve measures 48cm(19ins) or length required. Cast off **loosely.**

Neckband:
Join right shoulder seam. Using 4.5mm (UK7, USA6) needles, pick up 81 sts evenly around neck. Work 10 rows in k1, p1 rib. Cast off **loosely.**

Finishing:
Fold neckband in half and sew down to inside of garment.

Fold sleeve in half, place centre point of sleeve to shoulder seam. Measure down 29cm ($11^{1}/_{2}$ins) on each body side. Sew in sleeve loosely. Join other shoulder seam and sew in sleeve. Join sleeve and body seams.

Wash your natural jersey in warm water, rinse and roll in a towel to remove excess water. Lay flat to dry on a towel.

Winter warmer beret

Berets are great projects for experimenting with colour. They are quick and easy to make and there's always someone who needs one. I have used hand carded rolags of Ashford Merino and Corriedale slivers to create a light, airy yarn with a subtle blend of autumn colours. The rolags are fun to card and easy to spin.

You will need:
3.75mm double pointed needles, 3.75mm circular needle
Ashford Corriedale sliver: 25gm (1oz) of Nutmeg
Ashford Merino sliver: 12gm (1/2oz) each of Bean Sprout, Tangerine, Raspberry and Grape Jelly

CARDING AND SPINNING

As the fibre is already carded, a light blend is all that is needed to prepare the rolags. Place staple lengths of each colour across one carder, filling it to about the depth of the teeth. I used approximately twice as much Nutmeg as the other colours.

Brush lightly until the colours start to blend. Transfer the fibre to the other carder and brush lightly again. Roll the fibre off the carder and store ready for spinning.

Spin the rolags using the medium draw for a semi-worsted yarn. My plied yarn measured 15 wpi.

KNITTING THE BERET:

Cast on 8 sts and distribute on 3 double pointed needles. Place a marker to mark the beginning of the round.
Round 1: Knit into the front and back of each st (16 sts)
Round 2 and all even numbered rounds: Knit
Round 3: *K2, yo, repeat from * to end (24sts)
Round 5: *K3, yo, repeat from * to end (32sts)
Round 7: *K4, yo, repeat from * to end (40sts)

Continue increasing on every odd numbered round, changing to the circular needle when necessary, until there are 24 sts between each increase (192 sts). The beret should measure approximately 30cm(12in) across.

Next four rounds: knit

Decreasing for the brim:
Round 1: *K6, k2tog, repeat from * to end (168 sts)
Rounds 2 and 3: Knit
Round 4: *K5, k2tog, repeat from * to end (144 sts)
Rounds 5 and 6: Knit
Round 7: *K4, k2tog, repeat from * to end (120 sts)
Rounds 8 and 9: Knit
Round 10: *K3, k2tog, repeat from * to end (96 sts)
Rounds 11 and 12: Knit
Round 13: Purl
Round 14: Knit
Repeat rounds 13 and 14 three more times.

Cast off very loosely knitwise.
Weave in the ends and wash the beret. Block using a large plate.

Merino and silk scarf – pure luxury

A handspun, handwoven Merino/silk scarf is a very special and luxurious project for a handspinner. This is an excellent project for combining the carding and spinning skills you have learned. The carding is effortless and the spinning a joy.

To best show off the handspun yarn in this scarf, I used a 1/3 twill lifting which gives a weft-faced fabric on one side and warp-faced on the other. With only one shaft being raised for each pick, this scarf is quick and easy to weave.

I used hand spun yarn in the warp but you could use it in the weft instead.

CARDING AND SPINNING THE YARN FOR THE WARP

You will need:

50gm (2ozs) each of Merino sliver in Spearmint, Grape Jelly and Bean Sprout.

50gm (2ozs) of Tussah or Bombyx Mori silk sliver.

When blending luxury fibres together, it is more efficient to work with small batts. Large batts can become difficult to handle and the blend may not be as thorough.

Divide each of the Merino colours into approximately 3 equal portions. Divide the silk into approximately 9 equal portions.

Blend one portion of each Merino colour with one portion of silk following the instructions on page 46, passing each blend through the carder twice.

To prepare batts for spinning, use one of each colour of the blends side-by-side on the carder. Pass through one at a time, covering about a third of the drum with each one and overlapping a little.

Carefully remove the batt and stretch into a thin sliver ready for spinning. Now do the same with the remaining Merino/silk blends.

Spin two fine singles and ply together for a yarn that measures 22-24 wraps per inch.

3/1 Twill Warp Dominant

1/3 Twill Weft Dominant

WEAVING THE SCARF

Weave structure: 1/3 twill

You will need:

Loom: 4 shaft

Warp: 220m (227yds) hand spun Merino/Silk blend, 22-24 wpi.

Weft: 120m (130yds) Zephyr 50/50 Merino/silk from Jaggerspun (2/18, approx. 5040yds per lb).

Warp length: 2.1m (7ft). Includes loom waste of 30cm (12ins), fringe 30cm (12ins), 5% take-up and shrinkage.
Sett: 14 epi
Number of Ends: 90 (includes floating selvedge)
Width in Reed: 16.5cm ($6^{1}/_{2}$ins)
Finished length: 140cm (55ins)
Finished width: 15cm (6ins)

Thread the loom following the draft in Fig. 1 below.

Sleying:
For an 8 dent reed sley 1,2,2,2 for each half inch.
For a 10-dent reed sley 1,2,1,2,1 for each half inch.

Tie the warp onto the front apron rod, allowing 15cm (6ins) for the fringe. Weave a header with scrap yarn to spread the warp.

Weave 2 picks of plain weave then hemstitch around groups of 4 warp ends (5 at each selvedge). Continue weaving following Fig. 1 until you have woven 140cm (55ins) in total. Weave 2 picks of plain weave then hemstitch as at the beginning of the scarf.

Cut the scarf from the loom, being careful to leave 15cm (6ins) for the fringe.

Twist the fringes then wash the scarf by hand in lukewarm water. Roll in a towel to remove the excess water and lay flat to dry. Press the scarf with a warm iron while it is still slightly damp.

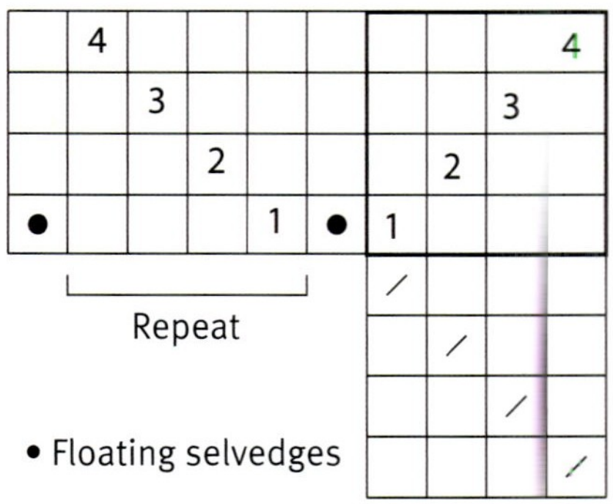

Fig. 1

Child's jacket

This delightful child's jacket is knitted in one piece and is easily adapted for different sizes and yarns.

To keep the colours vibrant and clear, each single is a different colour blend. This is a fun way to make a 2 ply yarn and learn about colour interaction. It is very worthwhile making a few samples as two different blends plied together can look very exciting on the bobbin, but quite different when knitted.

Size: To fit 18 months – 2 years

You will need:
Ashford Corriedale Sliver:
50gm (2ozs) each Lagoon, Lime, Tangerine, Peach
100gm (4ozs) of Ice
or five colours of your choice
1 set of 5mm knitting needles
Tension: 16st = 10cm (4ins) over stocking stitch.
Yarn: Spin a medium thickness yarn to equal approximately 11 wpi (wraps per inch) when plied.

CARDING:

I used the drum carder to make batts for a semi-worsted yarn. You could use hand carders to make rolags for woollen spinning if you prefer. Use equal portions of each colour in the blends.

FIRST SINGLE

Drum carding:
Use approximately 60cm (24ins) lengths of sliver.
First pass – blend Lagoon and Ice together.
Second pass – card the blended Lagoon and Ice, then add the Lime.

Hand carding:
Blend the Lagoon and Ice together then card in the Lime just a little.

SECOND SINGLE

Drum carding:
First pass – blend the Tangerine and Peach together.
Second pass – card the blended Tangerine and Peach, then add the Ice.

Hand carding:
Blend the Tangerine and Peach together then card in the Ice just a little.

Ply the singles together.

KNITTING THE JACKET

Back:
Cast on 50 stitches and work 9 rows in garter stitch (every row knit).

Pattern:
Row 1: Knit
Row 2: Purl
Repeat these two rows twice more.
Rows 7-10: Knit
These 10 rows form the pattern. Repeat 4 more times - approximately 20cm(8ins).

Sleeves:
Working in stocking stitch, cast on 8 stitches at the beginning of the next 8 rows (114 sts).

Next Row: Knit
Next Row: K5, Purl to last 5 sts, k5.
Repeat these two rows until sleeve at cuff measures 10cm(4ins).

To shape neck: Knit 48 sts. Place these stitches on a stitch holder. They will be used to work the right front later. Cast off 18 sts, knit to end (48 sts).

Fronts – Work each front separately

Left Front:
Next Row: K5, purl to end
Next Row: Cast on 12 sts, knit to end (60 sts)
Next Row: K5, purl to last 5 sts, k5
Next Row: Knit
Repeat the last two rows until sleeve at cuff measures 20cm(8ins) ending at cuff edge.

Keeping garter st edge correct at front opening edge, cast off 8 sts at beg of next and following 3 alternate rows, ending with right side facing (28 sts).

Pattern:
Rows 1-4: Knit
Row 5: Knit
Row 6: Purl to last 5 sts, k5
Repeat rows 5 and 6 two more times.
These 10 rows form the pattern. Repeat 4 more times.

Work 9 rows garter stitch. Cast off.

Right Front:
Place sts from holder onto needle.
Join yarn to neck edge, p to last 5 sts, k5
Next Row: Knit
Next Row: Cast on 12 stitches (60 sts), k5, p to last 5 sts, k5
Next Row: Knit
Next Row: K5, purl to last 5 sts, k5
Repeat the last two rows until sleeve at cuff measures 20cm(8ins) ending at cuff edge.

Keeping garter st edge correct at front opening edge, cast off 8 sts at beg of next and following 3 alternate rows, ending with wrong side facing (28 sts). Work 1 row.

Pattern:
Rows 1-4: Knit
Row 5: Knit
Row 6: K5, purl to end
Repeat rows 5 and 6 two more times
These 10 rows form the pattern. Repeat 4 more times.

Work 9 rows garter stitch. Cast off.

Collar:
With right side facing, pick up 12 sts from right front neck edge, 18 sts from back neck and 12 sts left front neck edge (42 sts). Work 20 rows in garter stitch. Cast off loosely.

Finishing:
Wash and block garment.
Join sleeve and side seams using a back stitch. Turn back collar. Attach ties at centre front where the stocking stitch yoke begins. A crochet chain, ribbon, cord or two lengths of the garment yarn twisted together would be suitable.

Novelty yarn scarf

Spin a knot yarn to make this easy to knit, brightly coloured scarf. The frequent colour change is fun to spin and the knots look great in the different colours. The ridges and medallions will show off your novelty yarn beautifully.

I used a combination of four Ashford Corriedale and Merino colours for one single, and black Merino for the other. The Merino gives the scarf extra softness for wearing next to the skin.

You will need:

Ashford Corriedale and Merino slivers:
100gm (4ozs) of Black - Merino
25gm (1ozs) each of:
Tangerine – Merino
Scarlet – Merino
Purple – Corriedale
Magenta – Corriedale
1 set of 5mm knitting needles
Tension: 10sts = 4cm ($1^1/_2$ins)
Yarn: Spin a medium thickness yarn to equal approx. 16 wpi when plied

SPINNING

For one of the singles, pull off a staple length of each of the colours, except the black. Divide each staple into four portions. Spin one portion of each colour either in the same sequence or in a random order.

Spin a second single of black Merino to the same thickness as the first one.

Make a knot yarn following the directions on page 79. For this yarn I made knots at about 50cm(20ins) intervals.

Wash the yarn in warm water with a liquid wool wash to set the twist.

KNITTING THE SCARF

Cast on 26 stitches.
Row 1: (RS) Knit
Row 2: Knit
Row 3: K6, *yo twice, k1, yo 3 times, k1, yo4 times, k1, yo 3 times, k1, yo twice, k6; repeat from * to end
Row 4: Knit, slipping all yarn over stitches off the needle
Row 5: Knit
Row 6: Knit
Row 7: K1, *yo twice, k1, yo 3 times, k1, yo 4 times, k1, yo 3 times, k1, yo twice, k6; repeat from *, end last repeat k1 instead of k6
Row 8: Knit, slipping all yarn over stitches off the needle

Repeat rows 1-8 until scarf is at desired length, finishing on either row 2 or 6. Cast off.

Finishing:

Wash in warm water with wool wash and lie flat to dry.

The Ashford Traditional Spinning Wheel

Spinning on an Ashford Wheel

The Ashford range of spinning wheels provides a tremendous choice for the hand spinner.

Whether you are a new or experienced spinner, there are several important points to consider when purchasing a wheel. Size, weight, versatility, portability and cost. If you know what type of spinning you want to do, the drive ratio will be another important consideration.

TENSIONING SYSTEMS

Single drive (Scotch tension): A single drive wheel has a single drive band around the drive wheel and flyer whorl. The drive band can be tensioned by either adjusting the knob, or by using a band made from polycord which is self-tensioning.

A separate band, known as the brake band, runs over a groove in the end of the bobbin and is attached to a knob located near the orifice end of the maiden. A tension spring is attached to the other end to provide an even tension. Turning this knob tightens or loosens the brake tension and regulates the speed at the which the yarn winds on to the bobbin. When the yarn winds on, the bobbin slows or stops still while the flyer continues turning. The higher the tension, the faster the yarn will wind on. The spinner has complete control over the tension on this type of wheel and can spin a large variety of yarns.

Double Drive: This system uses one continuous drive band which is doubled and crossed in a figure of eight and connects the drive wheel, flyer and bobbin. There is just one adjusting knob that tightens or loosens the drive band.

When spinning, the drive band slips in the bobbin whorl but when the yarn is allowed to feed in, the bobbin accelerates and pulls the yarn onto itself. More drive band tension equals more pull on the yarn. Less drive band tension equals less pull on the yarn.

The double drive system tends to result in a slightly firmer yarn with a more consistent twist.

The Ashford double drive wheels also have a single drive (Scotch tension) option.

Bobbin lead (Irish tension): The bobbin lead system has the drive band driving the bobbin instead of the flyer. The drive band goes around the drive wheel and bobbin whorl. The brake band runs over the flyer whorl. This gives an even higher ratio then the regular double drive system.

To use bobbin lead (Irish tension), the yarn must be strong enough to pull the flyer around otherwise it will break.

Elizabeth 2

A beautiful, double drive wheel particularly suitable for fast fine spinning. Ball bearings and a large balanced, intricately crafted wheel for easy treadling and relaxed spinning. Can be used as single drive or bobbin lead.

Includes 4 bobbins.

Wheel diameter	61cm (24ins)
Orifice	1cm ($^{3}/_{8}$ins)
Bobbin capacity	100g (3-4ozs)
Ratios	8.5, 11, 15 (18 bobbin lead)
Weight	9kg (20lbs)

Optional accessories:
Jumbo double drive flyer
Distaff
Quill spindle
Double treadle
Sliding hook flyer

Traditional

Choose single or double drive.

A horizontal, single treadle wheel for fine and medium spinning using the standard flyer and bobbin. Ball bearings for smooth and effortless treadling. A wonderfully versatile wheel suitable for all levels of spinning.

The double drive can be used as single drive or bobbin lead.

Includes 4 bobbins.

Wheel diameter	56cm (22ins)
Orifice	1cm (3/8ins)
Bobbin capacity	100g (3-4ozs)
Single drive ratios	6.5, 12.5, 17.5
Double drive ratios	7.5, 10 (14 bobbin lead)
Weight	8kg (17.5lbs)

Optional accessories:
Jumbo double drive flyer
Distaff
Quill spindle
Double treadle
Sliding hook flyer

Traveller

Choose single or double drive.

An easily transported, versatile, double treadle, upright castle wheel for all types of spinning. Ball bearings for easy treadling.

The double drive can be used as single drive or bobbin lead.

Includes 4 bobbins and built-in lazy kate.

Wheel diameter	46cm (18ins)
Orifice	1cm (3/8ins)
Bobbin capacity	100g (3-4ozs)
Single drive ratios	5.5, 10, 14
Double drive ratios	6.5, 8.5 (11.5 bobbin lead)
Weight	7kg (15lbs)

Optional accessories:
Jumbo flyer
Distaff
Quill spindle
Sliding hook flyer

Joy

A light, folding, very portable single drive wheel. When folded the flyer and bobbins fit into the frame and the treadle board folds flat. Spin anywhere, any time! Ball bearings for easy treadling. Suitable for all levels of spinning and all types of yarn. Ultra light at only 5kg (11lbs) and comes fully assembled and lacquered.

Choose single or double treadle.

Includes 3 bobbins and built-in lazy kate.

Wheel diameter	40cm (15$^3/_4$ins)
Orifice	1cm ($^3/_8$ins)
Bobbin capacity	100g (3-4ozs)
Ratios	6, 8, 11, 14
Weight	5kg (11lbs)

Accessories:
Carry bag

Kiwi

A compact, single drive, double treadle wheel, particularly suitable for beginners. Simple and easy to use.

Ball bearings for easy treadling.

Includes 3 bobbins and lazy kate.

Wheel diameter	45cm (17$^{1}/_{2}$ins)
Orifice	1cm ($^{3}/_{8}$ins)
Bobbin capacity	100g (3-4ozs)
Ratios	5.5, 7.25
Weight	5.5kg (12lbs)

Optional accessories:
Jumbo flyer
High speed whorl
Sliding hook flyer

Country Spinner

Designed to spin extra-bulky yarn. Huge 22mm (7/8in) orifice. Bobbin lead with one large 1kg (2.2lbs) capacity bobbin. Double treadle and ball bearings for easy treadling. Leather flyer brake.

Wheel diameter	46cm (18ins)
Orifice	2.3cm (7/8ins)
Bobbin capacity	900g to 1kg (2.2lbs)
Ratio	4.0
Weight	6.6kg (14.5lbs)

e-Spinner

A compact, quiet, portable electronic spinner suitable for all skill levels and all types of yarn. Incorporates a sliding hook jumbo flyer. Variable speed, 12v motor. Spin at home or on holiday. Assembled and lacquered.

Includes 3 jumbo bobbins and lazy kate with yarn guide.

Orifice	1.5cm (5/8ins)
Motor	12voltDC 6amp
Speed	0-1200rpm
Bobbin capacity	225g (8ozs)
Power supply	110-220 volts
Weight	2.8kg (6lbs)

Optional accessories:
12v car power cord

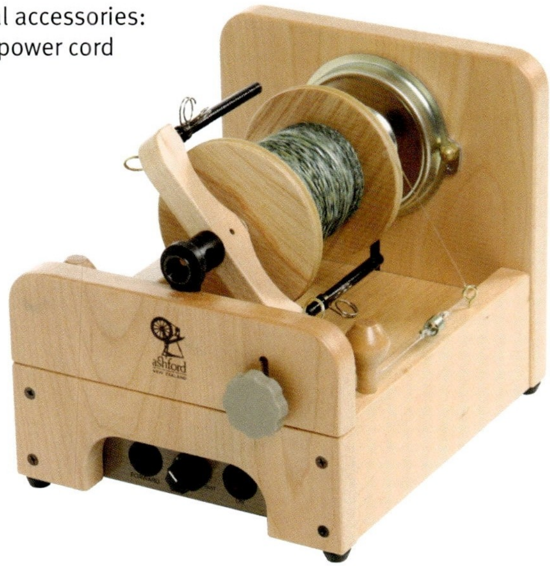

Your spinning wheel is a beautiful piece of furniture. Taking care of it will prolong its life and give you many years of trouble-free, enjoyable spinning. The Ashford Maintenance Kit contains everything you need to keep it well maintained and in top working order.

The Ashford range of natural timber spinning wheels are made from Southland Silver Beech, a beautiful native timber of New Zealand sourced from sustainably managed forests. The natural timber should be protected as soon as possible before or after assembly to avoid staining and provide protection from any climatic changes. Use the Ashford Wax Polish or any reputable wood oil or wax finish.

Factory lacquered wheels may be further enhanced with Ashford Wax Polish.

Before using your new wheel, or to maintain your current spinning wheel, use this check-list to ensure all moving parts are rotating freely and treadling is smooth and effortless.

The wheel, flyer and bobbin must all rotate freely.

Check by first removing the drive and brake bands. Apply Ashford spinning wheel oil, light oil or vaseline as illustrated on the opposite page.

Wheel

Spin the wheel. It should rotate freely.

- Wheel bearings (nylon only). Prise the wheel supports apart and apply a drop of oil onto the crank between the hub and bearings.
- Con rod bearing. Oil & check to ensure it isn't pinching.
- Treadle pins. Use either candle wax or oil to reduce noise and friction.
- Hinge pins on double treadle wheels. Oil as necessary.
- Check there is approx. 1-2mm (1/16in) side play between the hub & bearings. If the wheel is being pinched between the wheel supports loosen the bolts holding the frame or wheel supports until it is free, spin the wheel & then gradually retighten the bolts.
- Check that the gap between the bottom of the con rod (pitman) and the treadle rail is approx 25mm (1in). If greater than this it can cause ankle strain & if closer the two can bind thus stretching the joint.

Flyer

Spin the flyer. It should rotate freely.

- Oil the flyer bearings.
- Ensure the flyer bearings are at right angles to the flyer shaft. If not loosen the screws holding the maid upright, align and tighten.
- Check there is approx. 2-3mm (1/8in) end float between the flyer, bobbin & flyer bearings.

Bobbin

- Oil the bobbin bearings.
- If the bobbin doesn't run freely, apply a little vaseline or oil to the flyer shaft. If the bobbin feels too tight on the shaft, ream them with a 6mm (1/4in) round fine chain saw file or fine sandpaper wrapped around a pencil.
- If your wheel has been factory finished, clean any lacquer off the spindle.
- On double drive wheels the flyer whorls have "V" grooves. The bobbin whorl is "U" shaped. This difference enables the wheel to drive the flyer at a constant speed and allows the bobbin to accelerate or slow down when drafting. Check the bobbin whorl is smooth and "U" shaped.

Orifice

Dirt and grease will build up in the orifice, even with washed fleece. Clean regularly with a cotton bud dipped in methylated spirits.

Drive band

- Check the drive band is aligned with the spindle whorl. If necessary, loosen the screws holding the maiden bar, align & tighten.
- All drive bands stretch and wear out after many hours of spinning. Replace with either a cotton or stretchy drive band, or use the Ashford Turbo Kit and make your own stretchy cord to suit your wheel. The new band need only be tight enough to drive the wheel and no more. An overtight drive band will make treadling harder.

Hooks

Check the hooks on the flyer regularly and replace any that are worn or causing the yarn to catch.

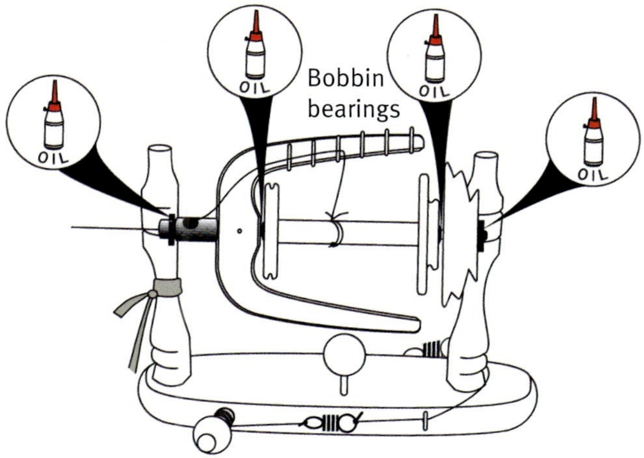

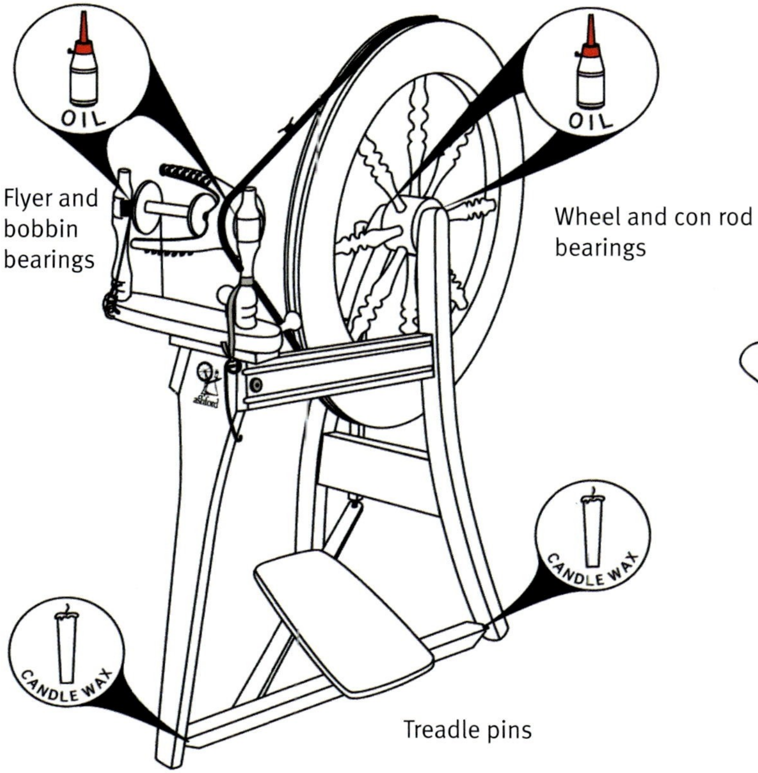

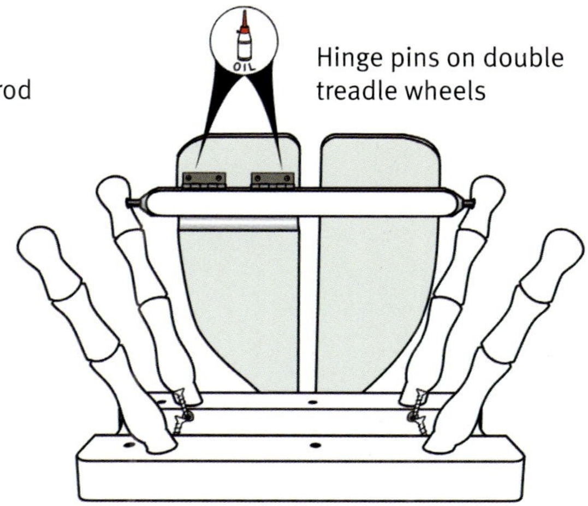

Ashford sliver colours

	Corriedale	USA Names
	001 Kiwifruit	Moss
	002 Jelly Bean	Navy
M	003 Cheesecake	Marigold
M	004 Green Tea	Fir
	005 Plum Duff	Eggplant
	006 Pumpkin Pie	Pumpkin
M	007 Spearmint	Teal
M	008 Grape Jelly	Lilac Haze
	009 Nutmeg	Nutmeg
	010 Bubblegum	Sky Blue
	011 Marshmallow	Rose
M	012 Strawberry Shortcake	Berry
M	013 Blueberry Pie	Periwinkle
M	014 Liquorice	Black
	015 Chilli Pepper	Chilli Pepper
	016 Grey	Smoke
	017 Peach	Copper
	018 Cookie	Camel
M	019 Bean Sprout	Lima Bean
M	020 Chocolate	Chocolate
	021 Blue	Blue
	022 Green	Green
	023 Magenta	Magenta
	024 Orange	Orange
	025 Purple	Purple
	026 Turquoise	Turquoise
	027 Yellow	Yellow
M	028 Scarlet	Red
	029 Skin	Cherub
M	030 Ice	Ice
M	031 Apricot	Apricot
M	032 Mint	Mint
M	033 Cupcake	Cupcake
M	034 Lavender	Sweet Pea
M	035 Honey	Honey
	036 Butterscotch	Butterscotch
	037 Toffee	Toffee
	040 Candy Floss	Candy
M	041 Indigo	Indigo
M	042 Lagoon	Lagoon
	043 Lime	Lime
	044 Lilac	Lavender
	045 Lemon	Lemon
	046 Pansy	Pansy
M	047 Raspberry	Raspberry
M	048 Tangerine	Tangerine
M	091 White	White
M	092 Natural Light	Light
M	093 Natural Medium	Medium
M	094 Natural Dark	Dark

Merino/Silk	
098 Juniper	Black Currant
099 Pomegranate	Pomegranate
100 Saffron	Mango
101 Cinnamon	Field of Rye
102 Peppercorns	Woodland
103 Salvia	Ocean
104 Mulberry	Mulberry
105 Poppy Seed	Poppy Seed
106 Spice	Spice
107 Damson	Damson
108 Vanilla	Vanilla

Sliver – washed, carded and dyed – is ready to spin or felt. Choose from fine Merino, soft Corriedale or luxurious 20% silk / 80% Merino blend

100% Pure New Zealand Wool

M *Available in Merino or Corriedale*

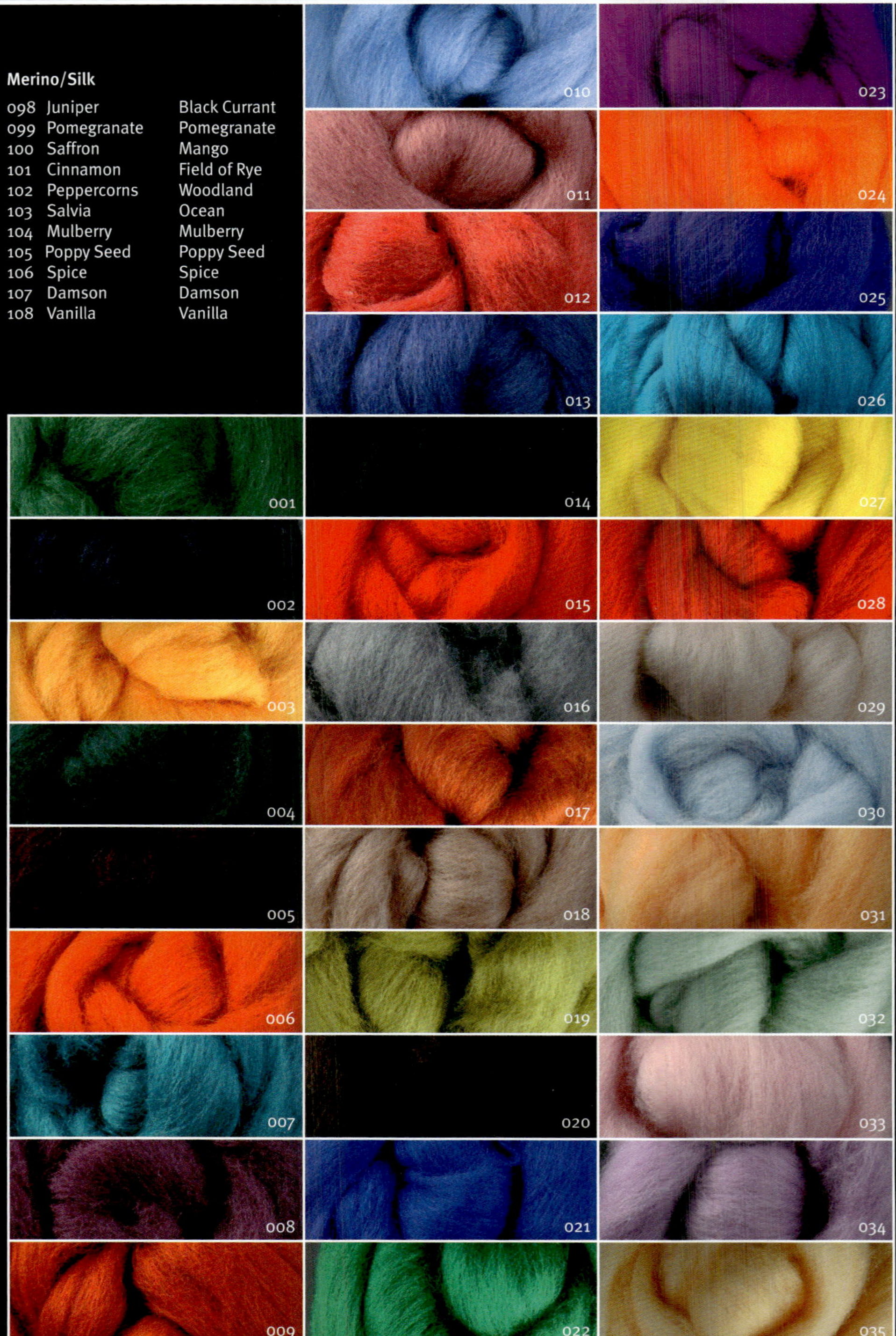

The Ashford Wool Sliver Story

Ashford wool sliver is made from 100% pure New Zealand wool grown on sheep farms in the North and South Islands. The farmers take great care to manage their flocks on magnificent wide open fields.

New Zealand has a temperate climate with a moderately high rainfall that helps wash the wool clean. And the clean grassy pastures ensure the wool is free of dust, dirt and thistles.

The sheep are generally shorn in early spring to encourage the ewes to take care of their new born lambs.

In the shearing shed, the farmers select only premium fleeces and skillfully remove any short or weak fibres, dirt or vegetable matter.

The wool is then carefully washed and dyed using ecologically-safe dyes (Oeko Tex compliant) in a beautiful collection of rainbow colours. It is then carded to align the fibres and blended to exacting standards

Ashford premium wool sliver is ready to spin, weave or felt without waste or further preparation.

Ashford sliver is available in 1kg (2.2lb) balls or 100gm (3 1/2ozs) bags.

It all started in 1934

It all began with a young man in the right place at the right time. However, the worldwide depression of the 1930s was not Walter Ashford's idea of a good time for starting a business.

But with purpose and determination he converted the family laundry into a tiny workshop in one of the most depressed suburbs in Christchurch, New Zealand.

Four days a week he worked making wooden fireside stools seated with seagrass. On the fifth day, with a stool on the handlebars of his bicycle, he rode the city knocking on doors and learned first hand that quality and value resulted in orders.

"Assemble and save"

Not long after this the Ashford family moved to Rakaia, a small country town. Here Walter rented an old building and set up a small factory. He repaired furniture and began making everything from picture frames to chicken coops. Good workmanship and modest prices brought their own reward. However, Rakaia's population of only 900 was hardly enough for potential growth. What he needed were customers. He gave it a lot of thought and eventually an idea came to him ... he would sell his fireside stools by mail order. Wrapping up stools and posting them presented him with a second problem, the matter of bulk. Then Walter had his second bright idea. He would make the wooden parts for the stools and post them together with an instruction sheet for customers to "Assemble and Save", a catch phrase that became the company's buy-line.

And so kitsets became a great success of the New Zealand scene. Because Walter was a practical man with a flair for design, his staff and production line expanded to include nursery and household furniture, utilities and toys. Walter's greatest assets were his ability to design simple practical products and the specialized machinery to make them.

The spinning revolution

In 1940 the Home Journal magazine asked Walter to design a spinning wheel that could make knitting yarn. It had to be aesthetically pleasing, functional, robust, trouble-free and yet a simple kitset that could be posted all over New Zealand. The first model was a double drive model, but Walter soon discovered that spinners wanted to change the bobbins with ease. So with the help of his father, the Reverend Dudley Ashford, the Ashford Scotch Tension flyer was developed and a patent pending awarded for its unique design. This revolutionary idea enabled the drive belt to be on the left of the flyer and it was just a simple matter of releasing the Scotch Tension to remove the bobbin. Today this innovation appears on many other brands of spinning wheel.

With World War 2 upon New Zealand, Walter's wheels were in great demand to create yarn for woollen socks and caps for our soldiers, sailors and airmen overseas. While Walter served in the Airforce, his father managed the business and with the help of a disabled foreman and a team of women, kept the factory working at top speed to produce 3,600 spinning wheels.

In 1945 Walter returned to his factory only to find that nylon, the new wonder fibre, was overtaking wool and hand spinning. It was over. For the next 20 years spinning slumbered like sleeping beauty.

Interest in wool revived

Then one day in 1965 Mrs Pamela Simcox knocked on the factory door and said, "Please Mr Ashford, make me 10 spinning wheels." This was not the sort of challenge Walter wanted to take up for the second time, remembering with distaste a storeroom of wheels, which had to be discounted at the end of the war. But Pamela persisted, emphatic that wool was the only wonder fibre, cool in summer and warm in winter. At agriculture and pastoral fairs, Pamela followed

Founder, Walter Ashford

the country's expert shearers spinning up the fleeces as they fell from their blades. She was persistent. Besides, why let that expertise go to waste? And so, once again Walter Ashford was in the right place at the right time.

Starting from where he left off, he saw the need to keep in touch with spinners, and by adapting, modifying and streamlining factory procedures he produced the popular Ashford Traditional Spinning Wheel. Still in the modest Rakaia premises and with little promotion, spinning groups mushroomed all over the country. Orders also began coming in from Australia, America and Europe.

A larger factory was constructed in Ashburton. Now, with plenty of space, machinery and skilled craftsmen, the manufacture of spinning wheels surged ahead. From these small beginnings Ashford have now produced over 500,000 spinning wheels and are exporting to over 40 different countries.

Quality, reliability and durability

The key to success has been Ashford's devotion to quality, reliability and durability. Only the best of materials are used. There is also a continual process of improvement and innovation in design, while retaining the aesthetic appeal of a graceful spinning wheel. The Ashford range of wheels allows spinners the ability to spin fine, bulky and novelty yarns from all types of fibre. As spinner, author and tutor Bette Hochberg has written, "Among my thousands of students, I have never met one who didn't learn to spin the type of yarn they wanted if they were using an Ashford. They are low-cost, easy, trouble-free wheels that spin all fibres in a wide range of sizes. They spin soft twist or high twist yarns, fast or leisurely."

It was only natural that weaving looms followed spinning wheels. Ashford now produces a complete range of high quality textile craft equipment.

Sustainable development

Since the beginning, the company's philosophy is to respect nature and work ethically and sustainably. The solid wood products are made of indigenous silver beech timber from Forestry Stewardship Council-approved mills. A business initiative to increase recycling and reduce the use of energy, water and waste was recognised with a regional Clean Green Award

While approximately 95% of today's business is with hobbyists and craftspeople in the western world, Richard and Elizabeth Ashford take great pride in their connection to communities which are less well off, where their spinning wheels and other equipment are vital contributors to families' wellbeing.

And of course, spinning and weaving are eco-friendly activities that reduce the dependence on non-renewable resources.

In 1986 Walter was awarded the Queen's Service Medal, a fitting honour for a man who gave a lifetime's dedication to crafts and his local community.

The family work is continued by son, Richard and his wife, Elizabeth who manage the factory, craft village and spinning wheel museum in Ashburton, New Zealand. Daughters Gay and Heather also promote the Ashford legacy.

Ashford Worldwide – in the Oman desert

Andean plying
A method of making a two-ply yarn from one source, usually the hand.

Balanced yarn
A plied yarn with an equal amount of twist in the singles and the plying.

Batt
A rectangle of fibre that has been prepared by a drum carder.

Bulk
The ability of fibre to expand.

Carding
The opening up of a fibre mass in preparation for spinning.

Carding cloth
A piece of leather or rubber material fitted with rows of metal teeth and attached to carding tools.

Combed top
A continuous length of fibre that has been combed in a parallel formation from long stapled fibres for worsted spinning.

Crimp
The natural wave pattern in staples of wool fibre.

Distaff
An attachment for a spinning wheel that holds fibre to be drawn out for spinning.

Doffer
A long, pointed metal tool used to separate fibres for removal from a drum carder. Also called an awl.

Drafting
The drawing out of a measured amount of fibre to be spun.

Drafting zone
The area of unspun fibre between the two hands during spinning.

Doffing strip
Metal strip across the large drum of a drum carder where the fibre is separated for removal.

Fleece
The wool from a single sheep.

Fulling
The washing and finishing process of a woollen textile.

Lazy Kate
A device for holding two or more bobbins during plying.

Leader
A length of thread attached to a bobbin for anchoring the first fibres when spinning.

Long draw
Method of drafting for woollen spinning.

Lustre
The natural shine or sheen of a fibre.

Medium draw
Method of drafting for semi-worsted spinning.

Micron
Also called micrometre or one millionth of a metre.

Navajo plying
A method of making a 3-ply yarn from an unplied yarn.

Niddy noddy
A device for winding yarn into a skein.

Orifice
The opening in the end of the spindle shaft.

Plying
Twisting two or more spun singles in the opposite direction to which they were spun to make a plied yarn.

Pre-draft
The drawing out of a length of fibre prior to spinning.

Rolag
A small roll of fibre that is the result of carding with hand carders.

Roving
Carded fibre which has been drawn into a long, thin strip with a slight twist.

Single
An unplied yarn.

Sliver
Carded fibre which has been drawn into a long, thin strip.

Staple
Naturally formed locks of wool.

Staple length
The natural length of a fibre.

S twist
Yarn spun in an anti-clockwise direction.

Short draw
Method of drafting for worsted spinning.

Woollen yarn
Yarn spun from randomly arranged fibres.

Worsted yarn
Smooth yarn spun from long staples of flick carded or combed fibre.

Z twist
Yarn spun in a clockwise direction.

In New Zealand where I live, we are fortunate to have an abundance of sheep. As a young girl growing up in this country, it was quite normal to learn to knit at an early age. My first project was adventurous for a seven year-old – not a scarf or a hat, but a jersey in double-knitting yarn. That jersey was the first of many, many more and the beginning of a life-long passion for knitting and wool.

It was an unusual event though that led me to a spinning wheel. While recuperating from a skiing accident, an Ashford Traveller wheel caught my eye in a shop window. I thought perhaps spinning my own yarn would be therapeutic and relaxing and might help to speed up my recovery. I bought and assembled the wheel, sourced a fleece from a friend who had a few sheep and taught myself to spin. I was instantly hooked - the whole process of making my own yarn was hugely satisfying and yes, it undoubtedly helped me to recover as I had something practical and rewarding to do with my time.

Now after 27 years my love for this craft has not waned in the slightest. If anything it is growing. Not only do I still get immense pleasure from spinning, opportunities have arisen to teach and nothing gives me more pleasure than to share my knowledge and experience with others. I hope new and experienced spinners will be inspired by this book and enjoy many years of spinning a good yarn.

Acknowledgements:

To Elizabeth and Richard Ashford – sincere thanks for asking me to write this book and for your support along the way. It has been a pleasure and a privilege.

To my husband Daniel Reeve, artist and calligrapher – thank you for your superb Illustrations. To Tina Gill – thank you Tina for your creative photography. I would also like to thank Graham Meadows for the sheep photographs on pages 54-61 (© Graham Meadows - www.gmpl.co.nz), Alison Jones for the image of her handsome coloured sheep, Jen Longshaw for the photo of her gorgeous angora rabbit, Kate Sherratt, Moira Youngquest and Nicola Bota of Ashfords for their support, Craig McKenzie for design and the models of course – Alice and Gareth Reeve, little Montana Davis, Lucy Ashford and Nicola Bota.